Sacred Sex, Sacred Life

Sacred Sex, Sacred Life

13 Secrets of Tantra

JANET LEE

Tendril Press

DENVER, COLORADO

Published by Tendril Press™
PO Box 441110
Aurora, CO 80044
303.696.9227

Sacred Sex, Sacred Life: 13 Secrets of Tantra

Library of Congress Control Number: 2010926724

ISBN 978-0-9841543-1-9 Paper

Copyright © 2011 by Tendril Press
All rights reserved

No part of this publication may be reproduced, stored in a retrieval system, or transmitted in any form or by any means, electronic, mechanical, photocopying, or otherwise, without the prior written permission of Tendril Press and Janet Lee. The material in this book is furnished for informational use only and is subject to change without notice. Tendril Press assumes no responsibility for any errors or inaccuracies that may appear in the documents contained in this book.

10 9 8 7 6 5 4 3 2 First Publishing: 2011
Manufactured in the United States of America on acid free paper.

Cover Image by: Helen Odland
Photographed by: Jarred Wegner

Author Photo: Arthur Despins

Art Direction, Book Design and Cover Design
Copyright © 2010. by A J Images, Inc., All rights reserved.
A. J. Business Design & Publishing Center, Inc.,
A. J. Images, Inc. Communication Design
www.ajimagesinc.com — 303•696•9227
info@ajimagesinc.com

*To Robin Taylor
in gratitude for the inspiration
to do this work.*

Tantra is a system of modern and
ancient spiritual practices
to promote health, happiness, and well-being.
Caution and common sense
should be used in following
any of the suggestions about food,
exercise, sexual activity, etc.
These concepts are all based upon
the author's experiences
and are not meant to replace
professional counselling
or medical advice.

Contents

Foreword ix

Preface xiii

Acknowledgements xxi

Introduction – What Are Tantra and Tantra Sex? 3
DEFINES TANTRA AND GIVES A BRIEF OVERVIEW OF WHAT MAKES TANTRA SEX BLISSFUL COMPARED TO REGULAR SEX.

Secret 1 – Be Willing 15
IF YOU ARE WILLING, YOUR WHOLE LIFE BECOMES VIBRANT.

Secret 2 – Be Present 25
BEING PRESENT IN YOUR LIFE AND YOUR BODY IS A NEW CONCEPT FOR MOST OF US. HOW CAN IT BENEFIT US?

Secret 3 – Fill Your Own Cup 43
WHAT MAKES YOU HAPPY? HOW DOES BEING SELFISH SUPPORT 41YOU?

Secret 4 – Prepare the Body Temple 55
LIFESTYLE CHANGES TO NURTURE THE BODY ALLOW HIGHER ENERGIES TO FLOW TOWARDS BLISS.

Secret 5 – Create Sacred Space 69
SURROUND YOURSELF IN BEAUTY AND PEACE TO BRING JOY TO YOUR HEART.

Secret 6 – De-Stress 75
LEARN THE DIFFERENCE BETWEEN GOOD AND BAD STRESS.81 PLUS 12 SIMPLE WAYS TO DEFUSE THE STRESS WE ENCOUNTER.

Secret 7 – Relax 83
ONLY WHEN THE BODY IS IN A STATE OF RELAXATION CAN IT HEAL ITSELF.

Secret 8 – Breathe 91
WE HAVE FORGOTTEN HOW TO BREATHE. THESE SIMPLE TECHNIQUES HELP US GET BACK IN TOUCH WITH OUR BODIES AND CALM THE MIND.

Secret 9 – Squeeze the Love Muscle 105
THIS IS THE MOST IMPORTANT MUSCLE FOR MAKING LOVE FOR BOTH MEN AND WOMEN. USE IT TO CREATE AN ENHANCED QUALITY OF LIFE FOR THE REST OF YOUR LIFE.

Secret 10 – Men are to Serve Women 113
WHAT DOES THIS MEAN? WHEN WOMEN ARE HONORED AND LOVED FROM THE HEART, EVERYTHING CHANGES FOR THE BEST LIFE POSSIBLE.

Secret 11 – The Masculine Principle – Ejaculation Mastery 123
ONCE YOU LEARN THIS INVALUABLE TECHNIQUE YOU'LL GAIN MASTERY IN ALL AREAS OF YOUR LIFE.

Secret #12 – The Feminine Principle – Doorway to Enlightenment 133
THE DIVINE ESSENCE IS IN THE FEMININE ENERGY. LEARNING TO LOVE WITH AN OPEN HEART TAKES YOU AND YOUR PARTNER TO BLISS.

Secret 13 – Conscious, Loving Communication 143
COMMUNICATION IS THE KEY TO ANY SUCCESSFUL RELATIONSHIP. WHEN WE RESPECTFULLY ASK FOR WHAT WE NEED, IT BRINGS JOY TO EVERYONE.

Conclusion 153

Glossary 157

Bibliography 159

About the Author 161

> "In choosing a lover,
> you are choosing
> your destiny."
>
> —Mantak Chia,
> The Multi-Orgasmic Couple

Foreword

As a teacher of Tantra since 2000, I have met many people seeking advanced training. Most are gung-ho to help others rather than find the teaching for them. Janet Lee was not that type of student. Her desire for self-healing and growth made her stand out. If you are seeking the same, you have found a woman willing to gather and share such information with you.

I first met Janet Lee when she traveled to Hawaii to meet me and learn advanced Tantric wisdom. Even though she understood that she was being led towards a life-calling, she felt confused about why she was embarking on such dangerous territory. Yet there seemed nowhere else to go. This is the way of many exploring Tantra. Is it about sex? Is it a religion? Or is it a Yoga? Tantra was leading her deep into the very questions many of us have.

Her journey is the work of the book you are holding.

With clear focus, she shares a core truth. She has always taken great steps to understand herself, knowing she could share this with others once it was time. She came to me as a seeker, but her true calling is a teacher…a teacher of Tantra.

There are many reasons to explore Tantra and the wisdom it offers. For most in the West, Tantra has been a collection of sex tips for the bedroom. The true gift in Tantra is it's an artistic approach toward life. Sex is part of life, and when we allow the adventure to explore the mysteries of life, ALL parts of our world grow and benefit. And as we become more aware, more skilled as lovers, we experience Tantra's magical impact on our lives.

Lovemaking is an art form in every way. If you want to have better sex, look at the effect of your lovemaking. How are you approaching your art? Every touch, every kiss, every word, every emotion is like a paintbrush stroke on your canvas. What are you painting? Intention and emotions are the colors. Actions and techniques provide the details created by the brush strokes. The experience and your lover are the canvas. Janet's book gives you a masterful approach toward knowing your body, mind, and soul. These are the very gems needed to create such masterful, artistic love.

The truth is, many people stick with a winning formula. They stay with techniques that have worked in the past. It's like an artist creating a masterpiece and reproducing the same work over and over again without any change. It may continue to sell for a little while, but then it begins to lose its appeal. We have to work and practice and stay creative in our lovemaking. The approach towards sex should not be lazy, but rather inspired with passion and bliss. We should learn to create remarkable sexual encounters that represent our lovemaking skills and allow us to pursue our desire for learning new techniques.

Today is the day to start treating life as the artist you are!

You are holding the key—the first step in your journey to unfold your mastery, the art of knowing you, your body, and how to share a richer sexual life completely with others. Tantra is more than just bedroom tricks; and Janet Lee has painstakingly created this guide as a path to help you reach into the very fabric of your existence and enjoy each day fully. Being a master lover creates a love affair with life itself. This is your birthright. Tantra celebrates you in this way and supports your growth, discovery, and liberation. Janet Lee's heart and dedication towards supporting empowerment, love, and depth are the very reasons this book is published for you to read. Enjoy the excitement as you read the ancient secrets now in your hands.

—SHAWN ROOP
MASTER TANTRIC COUNSELOR,
DAKA, AND AUTHOR OF

*PATHWAYS TO LOVE:
28 DAYS TO SELF LOVE*

WWW.TANTRAQUEST.COM

Preface

This book is only the beginning of a blissful life. Once you grasp the basics of great living and loving, there is no upper limit if you are willing to move forward to ecstasy in the beyond-beyond (past space and time into the essence of love from source—the divine).

Take what you like, do what you are able to do, and leave the rest. You have choice. Use what works for you.

The real secret is having an open heart to allow love in and to illuminate that love. The discipline of love is not something you can learn in a seminar. Love is hidden inside all human beings; it only needs to be uncovered. Most of us have covered ourselves with armor that does not allow love to surface.

Love is inside us. It is intrinsic to our nature.

This book is to help you be on your way to revealing that love. It starts with purifying the body, then working to quiet the mind, and ultimately connecting with spirit. This book is about understanding that sexuality and sex are the first rung of the ladder to enlightenment. Changing lust into love in our hearts permits us to move up the ladder until lovemaking becomes a prayer to the divine.

We are divine (spiritual) beings having a human experience. Once you have truly tasted the divine and felt the love that you long for, there is no going back. Many seek the genital orgasm and release only to be disappointed again and again. Love fulfills us and connects us. The cosmic orgasm is what we really seek. The first step is to love your body, for it is the temple of the divine.

We live in a touch-deprived society, yet a loving and caring touch heals. It connects you to your body, mind, emotions, and soul or spirit. Over years of giving bodywork, I have noticed that painful sexual issues affect our lives to the very core. Most of us have pain and want to avoid it at all cost. It tells you when you are out of balance, and only you can heal you. With awareness, a relaxed body, and a quiet mind, true healing takes place, and you can move into the state of bliss.

There are many ways to become transformed into an empowered being. Once you learn the 13 Secrets and how to direct the most powerful energy in your body, miracles happen. Love is sexual energy transformed. This book is the start of that transformation.

As you start to practice the principles, you will feel and look younger. You will feel connected to your beloved and others, and joy and love will radiate from your heart. The armor will gradually disappear. Living what is right for you and dancing to the beat of your own drum will create a an exhilarating life.

These ideas guide you to learn about yourself and your beloved. Exploring your heart and the ways in which you can love through sexual expression creates inspiration for yourself and others.

I am writing about sensuality, sexuality, and spirituality. Sensuality refers pleasure to the body or mind through the senses. It brings pleasure to the body or mind through all five of our senses: hearing, seeing, smelling, tasting, and touching. It also includes the sixth sense, which is spiritual knowledge.

> *Spirituality is not about being perfect but about aspiring to a life of heart-filled integrity. It is a journey and not a destination. When we are spiritually fit and balanced, we are a powerfully exquisite blend of human fallibility and divine perfection. It is this dynamic tension that gives us our uniqueness, our power to create, and our compassion.*
>
> —Caroline Reynolds

Sexuality is the physiological function that pertains to reproduction brought about by insemination of the female by the male through penile penetration of the vagina. I am attempting to take us beyond the physical act into a heartfelt, conscious, loving awareness that will move you to seek the spiritual aspect of sexuality to its fullest expression.

These *13 Secrets* applied in our lives can become more heartfelt as we gain confidence in ourselves. We treat ourselves and others with respect and joy. Our ordinary lives on the outside may remain the same, but inside we are filled with inspiration as we go forth to create the life we want—including a satisfying sex life.

The basis of sexual desire and its fleeting fulfillment is the ecstasy of orgasm, the most intense pleasure on the physical plane. When elevated to the spiritual level, one experiences union with the beloved. There is no separation, no "I" as apart from "you." In that moment of union between individual consciousness and the Cosmic, the anxious, striving, separated individual self becomes merged with the total flow of cosmic life energy, bathed in its unchanging quality of intense joy.

The orgasmic experience is available to all, and for many it is the closest thing to a mystical experience they will ever have. This momentary glimpse leaves us with a deep yearning to repeat it, not just for the sexual release, but for the truth it reveals, in that moment we remember who we really are.

In Tantra, you can extend the orgasm to last several minutes. Tantra provides a system of techniques to prolong orgasm, which allows us to experience Unity Consciousness. The state of bliss has been described as perpetual orgasm. Once you learn to attain this state in meditation, sex is no longer such a driving need. In orgasm, you are at one with yourself, with your lover, with all creation, with God or the Divine. There is no time, no past or future, only total presence in the eternal now. The breath stops, and the mind becomes empty. From this void, profound love, divine joy, and illuminating bliss emerge.

Orgasms can be achieved when we are inspired and passionate about life. The secrets of Tantra can become orgasmic if we choose to use them. I use Tantra as a means to inspire (which means "in spirit") others to be the best lovers they can be in all areas of life. I encourage everyone to be orgasmic with life!

Let's now begin the journey to an orgasmic life filled with mystery—to transform everyday existence into an extraordinary adventure.

Acknowledgements

I would like to thank Robin Taylor for all his encouragement and support while I was writing this book.

Thank you, Grant Mayor, Robert Baynes, and Dale Smith for editing my drafts and being constructive critics.

Thank you JD Sapra for your knowledge and skill as a published author and the encouragement you offered.

Thank you, Carisa, my daughter, and Arthur Despins for helping me with my computer setup and the encouragement you gave me.

From the bottom of my heart, I express deep gratitude to my Tantra Teacher, Shawn Roop, for his understanding and dedication to this practice.

Thank you to all my clients who submitted material for the book. Thank you to all who have waited patiently for its publication.

Many thanks to all who believe in me and my work.

Thank you to Tendril Press and the editing team for making it easy for me to get my book out to the public.

"Love,
enjoyed by the ignorant,
becomes bondage.

That same love, tasted by
one with understanding.
brings liberation.

Enjoy all the pleasures
of love fearlessly,
for the sake of liberation."

—CITTAVISUDDHIPRAKARANA

INTRODUCTION

What are Tantra and Tantra Sex?

TAN — TO EXTEND **TRA** — SELF

"TANTRA IS A HOLISTIC APPROACH TOWARDS LIVING LIFE AND FINDING UNION IN COMMUNICATION, EMOTIONS, SPIRITUALITY, PSYCHOLOGY, SEXUALITY, PSYCHIC ABILITY, SELF-HEALING, RELATIONSHIPS, AND MATERIAL SUCCESS.

IT SEEKS TO REMOVE THE DIVISION THAT KEEPS US FROM OUR FULL MAGNIFICENCE. IT SUPPORTS LIBERATION OF THE MIND AND BODY AS THEY MERGE INTO ONE. IT INCLUDES SACRED ART, MUSIC, MOVEMENT, ADVANCED BREATHING AND SO MUCH MORE."

—WWW.SECRETSOFTANTRA.COM

The word Tantra has different meanings. To me, it means technique, the method, the path. Tantra is not philosophy but a spiritual science. Tantra cannot be understood by the mind. Rather than an intellectual pursuit, it is an experience. If you are receptive, ready, vulnerable to the experience, it will come to you. As Osho defines it in *The Book of Secrets*:

> *Tantra is a spiritual science that works with action, in which every aspect of worldly existence is approached as an act of worship.*

Enlightenment can be found in all forms of activity, including sexual activity, and the practitioner's aim is to transform the everyday into the divine. In Tantra all the senses are harnessed, and the experience of ecstasy is sought as a spiritual tool. Desire is mastered, not through the flight from pleasure, but by total immersion in it.

Tantra offers a radical shortcut to spiritual illumination, holding that it can be attained in a single lifetime by cutting directly through ordinary awareness and conventional thought patterns. The everyday world of illusion coexists with the eternal, and enlightenment is achieved by realizing that each level of reality contains, and interlaces with, the greater transcendent whole.

It takes enormous courage and dedication to be Tantric in all areas of life including your sexuality. In a culture that is confused about sexuality, social pressures inhibit sexual expression. But you can never free yourself from sex by repressing it. In fact, efforts to avoid sex lead to obsession. Unexpressed sexual energy turns into neurosis and violence. Beholden to sexuality and yet not permitted to enjoy it, our hunger is never satisfied.

On the other hand, sex is thrown in your face in every magazine, movie, and television show. Base sexuality runs rampantly portrayed in our media culture, but there is

INTRODUCTION
What are Tantra and Tantra Sex?

little support for the idea that sexuality is an expression of sacred love.

Love is at the core of our very essence, and yet how seldom it is manifest! Western civilization has historically forbidden the expression of love by condemning sexuality. The contemporary world ignores love while exploiting sexuality. The Tantric practitioner must break the mold and defy the moral precept, for sex is one means by which humans come to know love. You can know the elemental truth of love by experiencing the divinity of sex and learning to worship through the senses, through the flesh. The more you embrace sex, the more free of it you become. Total acceptance and surrender to natural energies leads to sublime experiences.

What is the difference between mundane sex and Tantra sex? Nothing and everything!

Common sex is great; it feels good and allows us to connect to whomever we choose. It is pleasurable, passionate, and exciting. Tantric sex expands beyond the animalistic and instant gratification aspects of sex and takes it to a cosmic level where spirituality and sexuality merge and you awaken to profound experiences. It heightens awareness beyond normal levels and enhances overall well-being. Pleasure reaches new heights, and you can receive extreme healing, deep integration, and profound realizations. Greater possibilities of releasing limitations emerge the more you practice Tantric sex. Tantric sex provides an opportunity for core issues in our psychology to be eliminated so we may be in our full magnificence—the Divine state.

Physically speaking, Tantric sex allows us to extend lovemaking and deepen interpersonal connections. The teachings detail the benefits of surrendering and moving your energy, relaxing your body, breathing, and using sound while flowing in sexual union. Through awareness and non-judgment, it offers men and women a greater capacity to become multi-orgasmic. It reveals the role of intuition in becoming an extraordinary lover and calls us forward to use it.

Tantric couples worship each other as embodiments of the divine masculine and feminine energies. They employ lovemaking techniques to heighten and transform their sexual energy into the rapturous liberation.

Each of the these can become your spiritual journey. They are discussed in detail in the chapters that follow.

Prepare the Body: Your body is your temple, your gateway to the divine, and needs to be treated with the love and respect you would bestow on any holy vessel.

Prepare the Mind: Practicing transformational sex requires the cultivation of mind, body, and spirit. To appreciate our full sensuality, we need to quiet the mind and allow the experience to become divine.

Prepare a Sacred Space: To focus the mind and aid the harmonious flow of spirit during ecstatic lovemaking, you need to create and bless your personal sanctuary. This consecrated space will promote order and stability to anchor you both as you tread the threshold between the known and the unknown, and it will protect you by keeping out harmful energies. The preparation itself will be a profound act of creation.

Build and Share Sexual Energy: During the act of love, powerful energy circuits are activated. These circuits can also be developed independently, exchanged with your partner in non-sexual ways, and then consciously brought into your lovemaking sessions. Conscious breathing is an essential part of this.

Awaken the Senses: Far more than "foreplay," worshiping the divine nature of your lover is a sensual experience as you explore each other's body with tantalizing touch, discover erogenous zones, and harmonize your energies with sensual massage. Yoni[1]

---

1. Yoni means the female genitalia. In Sanskrit, it means the sacred garden, flower, alter, or space.

and lingam[2] worship are sacred and intimate acts that arouse sexual energy and create waves of erotic bliss as the energy moves throughout the body.

Channel Energy during Lovemaking: In sacred sex, a loving approach is far more important than technique. However, there are ways in which energy can be channeled more effectively. Channeling energy during lovemaking is as much about non-doing as doing. The "normal" sexual act is typically approached in a physically contracted state. When you relax and expand into your love and passion, sexual energy flows smoothly between you, building up the erotic tension and deepening intimacy.

To me, Tantra is the journey to enlightenment through applying sexual energy consciously. When one becomes aware, life is juicy.

Here is what one of my clients wrote to express his experiences with Tantra.

THE SIGNIFICANCE OF TANTRA IN MY LIFE

I was an ex-businessman in my late 50s and searching for some major new influence in my life to enrich my whole being when I met Janet

---

2. Lingam means the penis. In Sanskrit, it means the wand of love (not lust)

INTRODUCTION
What are Tantra and Tantra Sex?

Lee. With health issues forcing me to wind down a fairly successful business career and having been married over 30 years, I began to notice that much was lacking in the physical, intimate side of my relationship. At the time, I suppose that I was looking for more of a "quick-fix" from a traditional male viewpoint. My thinking was if I could only improve my sex life with my wife, then the world would turn in a much more meaningful way for me as I approached my golden years. How wrong I was.

After three years of working with Goddess Janet in her role as a teacher, mentor, guide, and therapist, I have come to the realization that the true key to fulfillment in a male-female relationship is the development of true intimacy. True intimacy leads to a feeling of completeness and satisfaction with one's self and one's partner— pure physical, sexual satisfaction does not. I have also come to better understand that truly and honestly connecting with a woman through the masculine heart is not an easy task. It is definitely a journey that will take most men a lifetime to understand (if we ever do).

So, let me describe what Tantra (and Goddess Janet) has meant in my life so far on the physical, emotional, and spiritual levels. First of all, in a purely physical sense, I now have experienced the world of multiple male orgasms.

Initially, I simply viewed this as an amazing and unique physical happening. But I now have come to realize that the true significance of physically experiencing multiple male orgasms is relatively insignificant. Once I finally understood that the whole point of Tantric practices are to connect (together) to a higher source—to get closer to the true source, from a spiritual level, I experienced how physical intimacy (if it even ever gets to this point, with your partner) can connect two people in an amazing manner. The truly life-altering part of this unique physical experience for me as a man was to better understand the complexity of the physical, sexual, and emotional world of a woman. Also, I now finally understand that there are male (lingam) and female (yoni) characteristics in each man and in each woman.

From an emotional perspective, even my very brief exposure to Tantric practices has allowed me to much better understand the unique differences in the male psyche vs. the female psyche. Until you understand how much it means to a woman to give herself completely to her male partner, you will never be able to receive her total love (physical and emotional) in the manner in which it is offered—truly, delicately, passionately, and selflessly.

INTRODUCTION
What are Tantra and Tantra Sex?

After three years of exposure to Tantric practice, I finally realized that I had, for most of my life, been living in a world of male-dominated thinking, a world of instant gratification and "taking." No wonder my physical relationship with my life-partner had deteriorated. I now realize that after years of believing that she was the source of my feelings of not being "complete," that I, and only I, was to blame for the majority of what was missing in my relationship, It was my lack of true understanding, my lack of patience, and my lack of "loving her from my heart." It had nothing to do with her, and it certainly had nothing to do with her lacking interest in sexual activity in the later part of our marriage!

From a spiritual level, I have experienced what I best describe as an "awakening." Over a period of a single week, including five very unique sessions with Goddess Janet, I experienced a totally life-altering "connection" and spiritual realization. I have connected with a higher level spiritually, and as a result, my impressions of my partner, my commitment to her, my love for her, and my understanding of her emotions and desires as a woman will never be the same again!

Whether or not I was in a dream-state, for me, this experience was very real, and my life will be improved forever as a result. I will no longer act like the typical alpha male, but rather as a complex human being who has both male and female characteristics and understandings (plus a weakening body). Where this "realization" will take me, I am not certain. But I do know it will be a vastly improved world for all the important people in my life.

—W.H.

The more I practice Tantra, the more I see a change in the quality of my life. My patience, acceptance, love for myself and others, peace, joy, and the ability to be more nurturing have increased a thousandfold.

I hope you enjoy these 13 beginning steps, secrets, to become the best lover you can be!

> "Genius of any kind is the ability and **willingness** to leave the known world behind and explore new territory."
>
> —Karla McLaren
> (American Author)

SECRET 1

Be Willing

> "A GREAT PLACE TO START IS TO BE WILLING TO BECOME AWARE AND OPEN TO NEW IDEAS AND CONCEPTS. THIS IS THE KEY TO TRANSFORMING YOUR LIFE."
>
> —WWW.SECRETSOFTANTRA.COM

Willingness is imperative. Without it you are stuck. When you are willing, old paradigms and thinking patterns are able to change or shift. Does that make it easy? No! Change and chaos go hand in hand, but with persistence, you can move through the "terror barrier" and transform. Sometimes, willingness is all it takes, and transformation happens as if by magic.

Without a willingness to explore and change, nothing new can come, and life becomes an endless cycle of dissatisfaction. This quote, often attributed to Einstein, says it well: *insanity is doing the same thing over and over again and expecting different results.*

The desire to change is akin to standing in front of a closed door. Knock and see if it opens. Behind the door can be anything you want in life. It can be the door to health, wealth, peace, fulfilling relationships, sexuality, new attitudes, harmony, joy, and happiness. You choose. Willingness is the *key* to unlock the door.

What does a door represent to you? There is a saying *"when one door closes, another door opens."* A door can represent new opportunities, a barrier, protection to keep others out, an entrance or exit, a means of access or approach. Does your door allow easy passage, or is it sealed shut, locked, or hidden? Is it a beautiful door, a broken down door, a door falling off its hinges? Does it creak and stick when it opens, or does it silently slide open with ease? Does it have a window in it or a beautifully carved doorknocker? What is it made of: wood, light, plastic, rock? What shape is it: rectangular, square, round, arched, narrow, wide, or two doors side by side?

Do you want to stand at the closed door? Do you want to see what is on the other side? Are you willing to go into the unknown? Are you willing to have a better life or live

Secret 1
Be Willing

life to its fullest? Are you afraid of what might be behind that door? Are you willing to go on an adventure? Are you willing to unlock the door and see the wonderful, beautiful richness behind it? Are you willing to be a conduit for the Great Creator?

Get visual. What does your door represent? Made of a beautiful heavy oak and carved with lovers surrounded by flowers and vines, mine hangs in an arched doorway. A rose knocker sits beneath the small window that allows me to see what is on the other side. Solid and sturdy, it opens with ease and grace. It has an old-fashioned keyhole and a carved rose handle. For me, it is a portal to higher levels of consciousness.

The mind and spirit work with images and pictures. So when we are willing, we create new pictures and cells of recognition.[3] If we are willing, we may open our minds to new levels of awareness and consciousness.

The first key to any change is to "be willing." The second key is to choose. You choose to be willing. Try the key. Does it fit the lock in your door? Does it turn? Are you surprised that it moved and you heard the click? Or are you

---

3. Cells of recognition are in the brain. Thoughts activate brain cells. When we become aware of our focus on something we hadn't previously seen or noticed, we develop cells of recognition. An example: you are planning to buy a new car. You decide on the color, make, and model. All of a sudden, you see that car everywhere even though you hadn't noticed it before.

disappointed because nothing happened? Whether or not you get the desired result, you are a success by just doing it. To me, there are no failures or mistakes, only lessons.

Let me tell you a bit about my journey to sacred sexuality. I made a decision after years of resistance to become a Tantra teacher. I understood there was a way to create sacred sexuality. I just didn't know how. This journey all started when I took a course from Marsha Wright-Sadoway called BodyMind Counselling. During the class, a section on values came up and we learned to identify our highest value. For me, this was easy. Spirituality is my highest value. What I didn't expect was to discover that sexuality is an integral part. It just happened to come up in a practice session. I went away seeing a new purpose in my life—sacred sexuality. I pondered it, looked for books on the subject, and searched the Internet. Everything I had read and heard about Tantra turned me off. It was not what I wanted to learn. But I was willing to learn and explore, knowing that my destiny was to bring sacred sexuality out to the world. Now I also recognize that conscious loving is part of this work for me.

My closest friends and clients knew all about my purpose and encouraged me. I took more training courses, one from T. Harv Ecker's "Peak Potential Quantum Leap" pro-

SECRET 1
Be Willing

gram in Vancouver, B.C. We had to tell an audience of over 500 people about our authentic self. I was willing to get up in front of others and talk about sacred sexuality. When I spoke, I felt everyone's heart open. The sensations as their hearts opened and no words were spoken were beyond anything I had ever experienced before. It was all on a higher energy level towards consciousness. No one questioned my authenticity or my purpose. I knew I was on track. I feeling compelled to go forward and learn more, I took a course from Tantra Quest, taught by Daka Shawn Roop in Hawaii. *www.TantraQuest.com*. Different from the other schools that had turned me off, his school is about uncovering and releasing one's core issues, especially around sexuality. Again, I was willing to step outside the box and face my own central issues.

Willingness is the key that has opened doors for me. My willingness helped me create my own website, put an ad in the paper, and start leading sessions. My partner and I had a booth at the Taboo—Naughty but Nice Sex Trade Show in Edmonton. We wanted to offer something different from the rest. With open hearts, we gave Tantra hugs to everyone who wanted one. We shared the beauty of slowing down and the sacredness that comes from sexuality. Some welcomed it, some ignored us, but we knew our willingness paid off when people thanked us for being there and shedding light on a taboo subject. Out of this experience, we started to offer workshops. It is all about being willing.

As you can see, being willing really does open doors. If I had stayed home and not taken any courses, I would have remained stuck. My willingness to open these doors has brought more joy than I had imagined possible. The more I research and apply what I learn, the more I am rewarded and the more others benefit. Their lives have been touched and transformed in some way, even if it is very small. A simple hug or soft kiss, or a light caressing touch, when you are open and willing, can lead to huge changes in your life that will surprise you—even to profound awe.

In a recent Tantra class I taught, being "willing" meant showing up as this class was done in the nude. If you can't be nude in front of others, this would not be a class for you. No one could hide, so judgments about bodies and sexuality were released, allowing a transformation to more openness. Each participant grew more loving towards their partner and others. They were amazed how free they felt and how this enriched their lives. Getting beyond sex or sexual taboos, participants learned to be natural, slow down, and enjoy life to its fullest. Each person that stayed with the class reported the experience helped them gain confidence in all areas of their lives.

One woman was very uncomfortable with this process. She did go naked with the group. She has since started her own business and is creating beautiful artwork based on her experience.

Be willing to move forward in your life. Don't kid yourself into thinking that standing still is an option. You are either growing or dying because there is no plateau or resting place. All creation is energy - everything is in flux.

It is now your choice to extract yourself from the cycles that trap and keep you stuck or move forward into a blissful and orgasmic life. Be willing to identify the patterns that have kept you stuck and choose to release them.

Here is a poem I would like to share with you.

THE KEY

WHAT GOOD IS A DOOR TO THE SOUL,
IF NO ONE GIVES YOU THE KEY —
NO ONE GIVES YOU THE WAY —
NO ONE TO HELP YOU TO SEE?

HOW CAN WE TURN TO THE LIGHT,
IF IN A DARK ROOM WE STAND?
HOW CAN WE FIND OUR WAY OUT,
IF THERE IS NO ONE TO HOLD OUT THEIR HAND?

Sacred Sex, Sacred Life
JANET LEE

> Why must we first lose our way,
> Before we stand still and reclaim
> All that in darkness we lost,
> If there's no one to call out our name?
>
> All these four questions are asked,
> By the many who stand behind doors,
> Waiting for someone to knock,
> Someone to give their lives cause.
>
> Intently look and make your eyes see
> That only when you ask the questions
> Will you understand what is to be...
>
> For the "Keeper of Light" will step forward,
> And your darkness and loss be no more.
> He will hand you the key if you ask for it,
> But it's you who must unlock the door!
>
> — Author unknown

The Law of Present Moment states that all power is in the present. You do not have any power in the past, and you do not have any power in the future.

The only time and place you have full access to your power is in the now.

— *Universal Laws of Conscious Creation Wisdom*, Lara Solara, Dana da Ponte, and Marlene Chapman

SECRET 2

Be Present

> "WHEN WE FEEL OUR BODY, THE SENSATIONS, THE PAIN, THE EMOTIONS, OUR FEET ON THE GROUND, WE BECOME ALIVE. WHEN WE EXPERIENCE TOTAL RELAXATION, OUR BODIES, MIND, AND SPIRIT CAN HEAL. RADICAL CHANGES AND MIRACLES CAN TAKE PLACE."
>
> —WWW.SECRETSOFTANTRA.COM

Be present! Be in your body. Be in this moment, the here and now. Don't think about the past or future. What does all that mean? What is *in this moment*? Only our undivided attention is in this moment.

Body presence is an uncommon state, for most people are 'beside' themselves or don't feel the ground when they walk or just have no awareness of their body at all. They only know they have a body when it is in pain, sometimes in a lot of pain. As my father-in-law is known to say, "If I didn't have any pain, how would I know I am alive?" Now in his eighties, he is always in some kind of pain. He values this because it indicates he is still alive and on this earth. What a way to be! I would rather be pain-free and happy, thank you.

We choose our thoughts. Our thoughts generate feelings. Our feelings lead to actions. Actions create the results we experience as "life."

THOUGHTS + FEELINGS + ACTIONS = RESULTS

Here is an example of a typical progression of thought to result:

Thought: I hate my job / I hate my spouse!

Feeling: Resentment, anger, and physical pain (migraine headache).

Action: Go to bed and sleep in a dark, quiet room for hours or days.

Results: A lower quality of life.

Here is an example of how this progression can shift when a person becomes more aware:

Thought: I hate my job / I hate my spouse! *What can I do about it?*

Feeling: *Emotions and physical pain can resolve as we recognize the issues.*

Action: *Introspection and exploration by going for a walk and/or meditating.*

Results: Change job or communication with spouse to become happier.

The result is a healthy, well-functioning body, free of pain and a life of fulfilment.

A male friend of mine whom I had known for over 30 years, recited the mantra "I hate my job" for years and years. All that time, he suffered with migraine headaches. I gave him massages to release his headaches before he went to work. Some days, I would get up at 5:00 AM to do this. One day, I asked the right question: "What is your dominant thought?"

He answered, "How much I hate my job." He hadn't realized his words and thoughts were causing his headaches so he could get time off. Once he recognized this, he quit his job and moved to China to teach English. His headaches disappeared. Surprisingly, I heard he is back in Canada, and guess what? He is working at the job he hated, and the migraines are back. Go figure!

Have you ever watched someone walking down the street and noticed they are not aware of their surroundings?

Sacred Sex, Sacred Life
JANET LEE

BAM! They walk right into posts. They even had their eyes open! They just float in la-la land. Most of us are in la-la land as we drive automobiles that can kill or injure others and ourselves. For example, my son does not know where his feet are. He walks everywhere because he doesn't have a driver's license. I thank God he doesn't; our roads are much safer this way. He has no idea how to let up on the accelerator pedal. It is 'pedal to the metal' all the time because he can't feel how much pressure to put on the pedal.

We occupy the body but are not living in it. We are beside it or somewhere else. It is a survival technique many of us learned as children to cope with extreme stress or things we didn't understand. Now, as adults, we still use the same coping mechanisms even though they are no longer effective. Squatters[4] or artificial demons[5] that we have created with our own thoughts set up house, and there is no room for us to return to the body. These new occupants cause us all kinds of problems: pain, obesity, forgetfulness, ill health, mental illness, etc.

If you ever had a trauma in your life, you may have disassociated yourself from your body. It is a survival skill. The

---

4. The term "squatters" is used when we leave an empty house or piece of land and an unauthorized individual occupies it in our absence.
5. Artificial demons called *egrogores* are created by our negative thinking and act like demanding children as we get older. They demand our attention and feeding with unhealthy negative thoughts.

trauma may be you were abused or mistreated. You may have even watched what was happening from outside your body. You were watching your body and what was going on. Some people experience this in near-death situations. This coping skill was needed at that time, but no longer.

Be present in your body and find something that fills your cup to move energy towards a healthy, vibrant life.

If you are not present and in your body when it comes to sex, you are short-changing the experience. Your partner knows whether you are in your body, whether or not you are attuned to your sexual energy. When the mind is elsewhere during sex, the penis and vagina know, and we end up with such things as a "limp dick" or a dry vagina. Have you ever had a sexual experience when your partner was there in physical form but emotionally or energetically absent? If you are having sex or making love and the other person is thinking about something else, such as a problem at work or what needs to be done around the house, or when is the next hockey game, can you feel that?

At a time in my life when I had four young children running around the house, my spouse wanted sex, but I was distracted. My husband asked on more than one occasion, "Where are you?" All I could think was: *It is very quiet all of a sudden. What are they getting into?* I was not in my body, enjoying the sensations or pleasure. My mind was with the kids.

Another way to put this, as Osho states in *Sex Matters: From Sex to Superconsciousness*:

> *Sex exists between two bodies; it can exist even with a dead body. That's what happens when you go to a prostitute. The prostitute is not there; just the body is there. The prostitute makes her body available to you, and she simply escapes from the body—because she never loved you, how can she be there? She becomes absent. That is the whole art of being a prostitute. She becomes absent to you; she simply forgets all about you. She may start thinking about her boyfriend; she may create a dream about her boyfriend, and she will completely forget you and leave the body at your disposal. It is a dead body. You can use it, but it is just a means. It is ugly, it is tremendously ugly, to make love to a dead body.*
>
> *When you love a person and the person is not present, or you love a person but you are not present, only bodies are there. It is a mechanical thing. When you love a person, you have to be present to the person; you have to be present to the presence of the person. Two presences meet, overlap, merge, and there is tremendous joy, there is peace, silence.*

Men are generally taught that the best way to delay ejaculation long enough to satisfy their partner is to think about

SECRET 2
Be Present

anything other than what is going on in the moment. This strategy kills off any potential for real fulfilment or satisfaction for either partner. When men do ejaculate, there is a release of tension, the hormone prolactin flows into the bloodstream making them want to roll over and go to sleep.

Ejaculate carries life-force energy, so it is worthwhile for men to consider what thoughts or feelings were present at that moment. Whatever you are feeling at the moment of orgasm and ejaculation will be absorbed by your partner. An orgasm that penetrates your partner's heart can be life-altering. Any negative emotions or thoughts will also be transferred.

Ask yourself about the last time you had sex. Did you come from a loving place? Did you fill your heart, body, and soul with such unconditional love to penetrate her heart with that love? A good way to tell is to see how the other person reacts or responds to you over the next day or two after sex. Are they loving and tender and joyous, or are they bitchy, moody, and angry? We may think we are loving and passionate and fulfilling our partner's needs and wishes as well as our own, but are we really? If you pay attention, you can gain some insight into why so many relationships suck.

A friend of mine was ending a relationship and decided to give this person oral sex as a farewell gift. He ejaculated into her mouth all his upsets and anger. She received mouth and throat ulcers that still show up from time to time. Nice gift to each other! It was a hard lesson to swallow. She became very aware at that moment what misdirected sexual energy can do to the physical body.

So, what does it take to move from mechanical sex to a fulfilling satisfying experience? First, of course, we must be willing.

Sex comes from the brain. Making love comes from the heart. Sex is motivated by the hormone dopamine[6], which acts like an addictive drug as it rushes into the bloodstream. Making love is a response to oxytocin[7], a bonding hormone and natural anti-depressant, released when we are feeling love. Sex is hurried, rushed, and goal-orientated while lovemaking is slow, sensual, and luscious—no expectations, no performance anxiety or goal driving to orgasm and release—a nurturing, loving, and relaxing experience for both.[8] When making love, feeling all the sensations can be overwhelming at first. In sex, feelings are obscured by the height of excitement, rigidity, and the rush of sexual

---

6. Dopamine is created in a gland in the brain called the hypothalamus—the brain's sex center. Men have a larger hypothalamus than women. Therefore, women do not have the same sex drive as men.

7. Oxytocin is the bonding and natural anti-depressant hormone that is released when you are touched in a loving way such as light caressing. It will increase desire, especially in women.

Secret 2
Be Present

energy. Since this is all we know, it seems satisfying. But is it really?

An erect, hard, aggressive penis creates a rigid, tight, angry vagina. Both lose their sensitivity over time and need more and more stimulation to remain aroused until, eventually, there is just numbness. The raw, coarse, and rough energy of sex blocks the ability to perceive the subtle, finer energy of a higher vibration. A higher vibration brings more awareness. Greater awareness opens you to higher consciousness, which moves you to enlightenment and empowerment.

Awareness heightens intuition and enhances health and happiness. Like a finely-tuned automobile that purrs and moves with grace and ease, you move through life in a state of bliss.

Feel the soft, sweetness of the yoni—the silkiness, the slipperiness, the energy of love. A softer lingam is less aggressive, and it is more sensitive and highly attuned. It can pick up the subtle movements of the yoni as it surrounds the lingam and caresses and loves it. Its nectar can then be absorbed and felt in the lingam as it moves through and up to the heart. The sensations are delicious, the heart

---

8. To a man, sex and love are separate. To a woman, sex and love are connected. For a man to know the difference and please his woman, he needs to slow down.

opens, and love can be sensed. We feel connected, moving towards oneness.

I believe we all want to be loved and loving. We crave that feeling and the sense that we belong. When we feel loved, we feel whole and holy, complete, nurtured, cared for, and connected to Source. We *feel*. We resonate all the vibrations around us.

Slow down. Stop. Allow yourself to receive. Allow yourself to give totally from love and your heart. Be conscious of touch. Feel how it can energize your body. Your body is your sexual vessel. Keep filling it to overflowing with love and creative energy. Spirit is turned on by expansion and growth and turned off by shrinking and disintegration. We are either expanding or contracting. Sexual energy can grow and expand and fill your cup to overflowing to bring wealth and riches in all areas of your life. The rest of our life will be wonderful if we know how to make love all day long from our hearts

Lovemaking is what God or Spirit is all about. Love is the most powerful energy in all of creation. Creating our golden orb of love energy fills us up to receive love, bliss, and peace. The mind loves the tension and excitement of drama and trauma. Yet, our true self craves peace. Too much excitement and stress burns us out, and we become dead inside. Eventually, it will 'kill' us in some way. Listen to what your body is saying. Listen to it if there is pain. Pain is your friend; it tells you that you are out of harmony and balance. Pay attention rather than avoiding it. Be willing to go through the pain to the other side—pleasure.

Feel your emotions as they come up, but don't *become* the emotion. Emotions aren't right or wrong, they just are. Feel them totally, and let them run through you. Blocking the feeling or pretending it isn't there creates *dis-ease*. Flow and movement of emotion allows it to pass quickly and puts us back in harmony. We are sentient beings. We are emotional beings. We are sexual beings. *We feel*! That's what makes us human. What would sex be like if there were no sensations? Would you still do the act? Would you find pleasure? No feelings. What would that be like for you? No emotions, no feelings, no sensations, no tingling, no excitement, no vibrations, just deadness. Think about it. Are some of you there already? Are you dead from the neck down? Are you a walking corpse or zombie?

Feel what touch does for you. Feel the softness, the textures, the vibrations, the electrical charge. Feel your heart and love. Feel the beauty. Feel the wonder of your body and the body of someone else. Can you melt into someone and become one with them? Feel their blood rushing through your veins? Feel so connected you become one energy source and orgasmic with the universe.

Feel the sexual energy. It starts out in the groin usually for men and in the breasts for women. Does it tingle? Is it hot or warm? Does it vibrate or pulse? Does it remain there or can you move that energy through your whole body and beyond?

In my work, I get people to first feel their sexual energy and ask those questions. Then I do a sensual massage with different strokes—masculine (short, sharp, staccato, tapotement or tapping) and feminine (light, flowing, barely touching or not touching at all—blowing on the skin or moving my hands a couple of inches above the body). This stimulates and relaxes the body at the same time. The parasympathetic and sympathetic nervous system work together, enabling the person to feel expanded and diverse sensations. They can feel the sexual energy move through the body. We do some "peaking," a term used when you almost are ready to orgasm or ejaculate and you stop, breathe, and bring the energy down a bit. Each time we peak, the client receives more vibrations, and finer sensations. When I run my hands over the body without touching it, a person can have body and heart orgasms just by this simple, loving non-touch. They feel the energy. They are energized—aware, alive, awake, and deeply moved. They feel new sensations in all areas of the body. They feel energy. They feel love. They feel honored and connected. They are happy and blissful, yet no sexual interaction was involved.

Most of my clients are surprised when they learn that I did not physically touch their body, because it felt like I did, and they are even more surprised at the peace and contentment they feel after a session.

Feel and be in your body. Go within and feel the sensations. You will be pleasantly surprised at how good it can feel. Often pain will disappear when you pay attention to your feelings and sensations. When you get out of your head and back into the body and heart center, lovemaking becomes a new, delightful game and a way of higher being that keeps going higher and higher. There is no upper limit to the pleasure and sensations one can feel. It will take time to perceive these subtle sensations and vibrations, but it is well worth the wait and effort.

Go for a massage and get back into your body. Walk in nature and feel the earth beneath your feet. Do some kind of physical activity—dance, skip, run, skate—something you enjoy. Hold hands and touch someone lovingly and consciously. Hug with a conscious loving intent. Feel your own body and skin when you bathe or shower. Attune to the sensations. Notice what feels good and what doesn't. Be present. You will be aware of so much more. Colors will be brighter. You will have more energy to do the things you want. You will feel alive! Enjoy the sensations! Be in your body!

Now observe your mind. Watch your thoughts. When we are thinking of the past or futurizing,[9] we are not in the present. We only have this moment. What we do in this moment determines the future. Once this moment is gone, it is gone. Do we do our best with this moment? I waste lots of time and energy dwelling on the past. This brings up feelings of guilt and a fear of the future that can create anxiety. When I can look at the past, see what lesson I learned, I move forward with the intent not to repeat the lesson. If I keep repeating the lesson, I haven't learned it yet.

One of my biggest lessons to learn is to say NO and mean it. I still haven't got that down yet. It is coming slowly. When I can't say no, I am in the past or feeling I will miss out. That is not true. Opportunity will come around again, and it will be okay.

Our thoughts are always there. They are always present. It is what we do with the thoughts that matters. The past is gone and the future will be guided by what I am do-

---

9. A term coined by Dr. Gerald Epstein–*The Natural Laws of Self-Healing*. It means when thoughts go into future events and create fear or anxiety.

Secret 2
Be Present

ing in this exact moment. I am writing. This is taking me to where I want to go—to complete and have a finished book for you to enjoy. This allows me to share my skills and knowledge with you.

To be successful in your life, be present. Feel what is going on in your body, and in your heart. Focus your mind at all times. The level of peace in your heart is the navigator that tells you whether or not you are on track in your life. Be present in this moment.

Sacred Sex, Sacred Life
JANET LEE

"What brings you pleasure? Do it, and do it often, for it will give lightness to your heart and do wonders for your soul."

CHERIE CARTER-SCOTT, PHD.
IF LIFE IS A GAME, THESE ARE THE RULES

Secret 3

Fill Your Own Cup

> "WHAT GIVES YOU JOY?
> WHAT FILLS YOU UP WITH THE ENERGY?
> WHAT EXCITES YOU?
> WHAT FIRES UP YOUR PASSION?
>
> FILL YOUR CUP FIRST TO OVERFLOWING
> TO CREATE A PEACEFUL AND HARMONIOUS LIFE.
> THE OVERFLOW THEN CAN BE USED FOR OTHER THINGS
> SUCH AS RELATIONSHIPS, WORK, PLAY, SUCCESS,
> MANIFESTATION, FAMILY, FRIENDS..."
>
> —WWW.SECRETSOFTANTRA.COM

When I've asked myself the above questions, the first answer that pops up is 'sex.' Most people think about sex at some point in their day. Everyone is interested in sex. Sex is always in the mind and on the mind, forming a central theme in our thoughts and daydreams.

But how many of us really don't know what gives us joy and makes us happy or fills us with energy? We live in such a fast-paced, stressful society that we have forgotten what gives us pleasure and energy. We have left our bodies and can't sense or feel anything. We have become numb and indifferent.

Small things can fill our cup. I love receiving flowers. They brighten my day and the days that follow. They create beauty in my environment, and beauty fills my cup. Tidiness and order fill my cup by creating space for new opportunities to come in and bringing order to my mind. This, in turn, gives me a sense of peace because no energy is wasted in looking for things. The sun produces the Vitamin D, which we need to stay healthy. Even 15 minutes of sunlight a day helps me to stay focused and be happy. Lack of sunshine leaves me sad and depressed.

For me, the thing that really fills my cup to overflowing is teaching and sharing information, planting seeds of awareness. After I have given a massage or talked to someone who is open, or taught a class, I feel energized and alive. I have a sense that vital energy has overflowed into the other person's life so they, too, can feel alive and move forward with their dreams and life purpose.

When we don't fill our cup, or we fill it up and then tip it over into someone else's cup, we rapidly become depleted. With our energy and vitality drained away, we feel used, abused, stressed, and/or exhausted.

Everything you do is either giving you energy or sapping your energy away (your job, your relationships, your house,

SECRET 3
Fill your own Cup

your stuff, your pets, etc.). Know what depletes your energy so you can replace them with things that will attract an abundance of joy and great opportunities into your life and generate even *more* energy for you.

Here is an exercise for you to do. Write down 50 or more things that you are currently *tolerate* in your life. Prioritize the list and address each one until you've eliminated 80% of them.

Seeing litter when I take my walks really saps my energy. So I carry a big garbage bag with me and pick up the trash as I go; this is my way of doing community service. I get exercise bending over—a bonus—and there is less litter. Some days, I really enjoy my walks because I don't find anything I need to pick up.

This is how my Tantra teacher, Shawn Roop of Tantra Quest, explained the cup theory to me;

Imagine three cups. The first cup represents you, the second cup represents another person or thing, and the third cup represents the relationship between the two. We each are responsible for filling own cup. The relationship energy includes two people or a person and a thing (for example: money, car, house, career, etc.) You have a relationship with all things and all people. Each creates a cup.

Now, if I fill my cup up with the things I enjoy, I have choices as to how I use my energy. I can empty it into someone else's cup (which will not be used for my higher good or that of the other person), or I can overflow it into the relationship cup, or I can dump it into "No Thing." Let me illustrate: My cup is ¾ full and you are feeling tired and crabby or ill. If I feel obligated to pamper you and do things for you out of guilt, I fill your cup and deplete mine. You will feel better for an hour or two, or maybe a day or two, and then your cup will be empty again. My cup was drained because my giving generated resentment inside of me. This kind of exchange won't really help you or me. You didn't fill your own cup; instead, you let me do that for you, and it didn't satisfy you or sustain you. Now, we are both depleted, the relationship is depleted, and no one wins or gains energy. Anger, depression, bitterness, or arguments can be the result.

Now, if you fill your cup doing things that you love, and I fill my cup doing things I love to do, our vitality and life force become strong. We are confident, healthy, and have a respect for each other. When our energy flows fills other cups or the relationship cup, we don't feel depleted or deprived. With loving respect for ourselves and the other person, we do things together that make us feel good and make the relationship stronger. We become more loving; the relationship grows and flourishes. Our growth and fullness of life provides the time and energy to be with

SECRET 3
Fill your own Cup

the other person or thing and create energy that moves us forward. This becomes a co-creative relationship.

When I fill my cup to overflowing and it flows into the relationship, but the other fails to fill his/her/its own cup, the relationship loses its balance. The parties aren't growing together when only one is doing his/her part, and the relationship is doomed to fail. Say that two people share a car they both drive, but only one refills the tank with gas. Eventually, the one doing the refuelling becomes resentful or even runs out of money to buy the gas, so no one fills the tank. The car won't go very far on empty.

This principle works in our relationships with things. I had a friend who owned a truck named 'Chico.' He took great care of it. He loved that old truck and took great care of it. It was old but in great shape. If he lent it to someone else, it would break down. Something would go wrong, and it refused to move. As soon as the owner got in, it ran beautifully. They had an exclusive love affair.

My relationship with my car is great as long as I keep the gas tank above one quarter. However, I was neglectful and let it go down too far. One night, the fuel pump broke, and I was stuck in the middle of one of the busiest intersections in the city. I learned I need to keep up my end of the relationship with my car, or it will stop at the most inconvenient times.

Everything we relate to will receive our life-force energy —good, bad, indifferent—whatever or however you feel will flow into the object or person.

It is vitally important to know how to fill your cup to overflowing. Know your passions. Have hobbies, love your work, do fun activities, get enough rest.

Don't give your energy away, especially where it is not wanted and where it will not be appreciated. I will give you an example. I teach Reiki. One of the principles addresses the need to do everything with an exchange of energy. That might mean I receive money for a session or that someone makes me cookies as payment. If I choose to do the session as a gift, there is no attachment to the energy I used. I cannot feel resentful if the client does not appreciate the gift of healing I gave them. We are taught not to throw our pearls before swine. That means we don't give away energy where it is not wanted or valued. Some people do not want to get better. We have to respect their wishes. We can ask permission or offer suggestions, but to impose our views on others is a poor use of energy that will deplete our cup and theirs.

Do something every day to fill your cup. Take a day off once in awhile to fill it to overflowing. As I am writing this, I am sitting in the sunlight outside, enjoying every moment. I feel energized, refreshed, content, happy, alive.

Secret 3
Fill your own Cup

I sense the world around me and am focused on what fills my cup.

When we do things that drain our energy, we feel unhappy, stressed, fatigued, depressed, even physically ill. We escape our bodies, retreating to a place where we cannot focus or think clearly. We are a mess!

Notice as you go through each of your daily activities: does it give you energy, or does it drain you? There is a motto I use to keep my energy up:

> 'I LOVE WHAT I DO,
> AND I DO WHAT I LOVE.'

Some tasks must be done whether we like it or not. If I am doing something I don't relish—like washing dishes—I make it a game. I challenge myself. I may improvise a new way to cut down the washing time or use less water. New thoughts and ideas come in, and sometimes I even catch myself having fun, being creative. I feel alive and energized.

Any task can give you energy if you apply an attitude of gratitude. I once heard a story about a tollbooth worker. Happy and smiling, he had his music blaring and he was dancing up a storm. He invited each driver as they paid the toll to join his party. When asked why he did what he did, he responded, "What better way to get paid? I'm having a party every day and dancing!" He turned his 'job' into a party. He knew how to fill his cup. What energy do you think he got from that? Lots! His life overflowed with fun and joy. Maybe we could all learn something from this young man.

Before I leave this subject, I want to go back to sex. Most men I have worked with say sexual release gives them energy and they want to 'take' that from their woman. Why? It makes a man feel good. At the same time, the woman is probably tired, bitchy, and nagging because she is depleted from the man's "taking". A man says, "But I am giving her pleasure first so she feels wonderful and has an orgasm. Then we have sex so I can ejaculate."

Really? What that means is this: it gives him pleasure to pleasure her, thinking all the time he is going to *get* his release. While he thinks his loving passion is "giving," really he is taking. It is tricky.

Can you give totally and freely without thinking of yourself for a moment? Can you just give without thoughts of taking or "what is in it for me?" Can you just receive without feeling you have to give back? This is hard to do. In my work, I find that getting men to "receive" is difficult. They feel they have to touch me or do something. They are so afraid just to enjoy and receive pleasure. This does not

SECRET 3
Fill your own Cup

mean we should only receive. We need to balance giving and receiving. This is what Tantra is about.

One of my clients was amazed to realize how good it feels to slow down and just receive. When he first came to me, he was obsessed with having sex two or three times a day. In his late fifties and retired, his sexual encounters with his wife lasted about five minutes each time. When I asked him about foreplay, he asked what that was. WOW! I had a lot of work ahead of me. With his wife's blessing, we started practicing spooning. He felt loved and honored. Now he is serene, and people have noticed he doesn't fly off the handle when things don't go well. He is kinder and finds great satisfaction in the new closeness he shares with his wife. Even his son is communicating with him, which was not the case before.

Conscious loving is a new way of being: fill your cup, be in your body, feel your feelings, observe all the while. Communicate with your partner. Describe your body sensations. Listen as your partner shares his/her feelings and describes the same body sensations. When both cups are being filled with this sexual energy, a third "entity," or cup, is created to receive the overflow, creating a new energy field and resource for both. With this comes a higher level of awareness and blissful ecstasy, which explodes into all three cups.

All cups are filled, happy, content, and peaceful. Now passion becomes a source of energy. Rather than feeding off each other, you have filled all the cups together.

The cup theory makes these energy concepts easier to visualize. Once you understand and practice it, it will change your life.

Women usually give and give and give until they burn out or get sick. Some men do the same. Learning to receive is also a way to fill your cup. When you give and receive in balance, your life will attract more of what you desire.

Life's purpose is love—to be happy, full of joy in every area of your life and connect with the divine source. Fill your own cup with things you love to do to the point of overflowing and let that be used for the other projects and people in your life.

There is only one
temple in the world,
and that is
the human body.

Nothing is holier than
this high form.

One touches heaven
when one touches
a human body."

—NOVALI

SECRET 4

Prepare the Body Temple

> "YOU WILL RECEIVE A BODY
> FOR THE DURATION OF YOUR TIME HERE.
> LOVE IT OR HATE IT, ACCEPT IT OR REJECT IT,
> IT IS THE ONLY ONE YOU WILL RECEIVE IN THIS LIFETIME.
> THERE IS NO-REFUND OR EXCHANGE POLICY.
> IT IS YOURS TO KEEP."
>
> —CHERIE CARTER-SCOTT, PHD
>
> *IF LIFE IS A GAME, THESE ARE THE RULES.*

Your physicality is as holy as any other aspect of your being. Honor your body as an extension of your soul. Enjoy its beauty, its imperfections, its capacity for pleasure, its vigor and vitality.

A Tantric lifestyle celebrates the joys of life, yet seeks to maintain a state of harmony within it. Health and happiness flourish when you bring greater awareness to all your daily activities. Find the right balance between rest and activity, pleasure and work, body and mind, intellect and spirit. Fundamental to this holistic approach is the food you eat. Food not only forms your physical body, but also influences your mind, thoughts, and emotions. It affects your sexual sensitivity and even the taste and odor of sexual secretions.

The human body is like a magnificent steed that carries the mind wherever it wants to go. It is a perfect servant, an outward projection of your attitudes and feelings. If you saw someone deliberately abusing such a fine animal, feeding it poison, denying it water, contaminating its air supply, confining its movement, or ignoring its need for affection, you would be outraged! Notice how you treat your body.

This situation continues because of your unconsciousness. You do not honor yourself enough to take care of yourself, or you have a hidden agenda—even a death wish. You may choose toxicity as a way to hold your consciousness at a lower level. Toxicity and the resulting lethargy and poor health are effective distractions and deterrents to spiritual awakening.

You can control many harmful factors with filters for air and water, healthy food choices, regular exercise, avoiding drugs, etc. More importantly you can live healthily in a polluted environment, even survive an epidemic, by maintaining body consciousness and holding a high vibration. A healthy lifestyle that enhances consciousness inspires further improvement, creating an upward spiral.

Secret 4
Prepare the Body Temple

Tantra and other ancient yogic traditions divide food into three types: sattvic, rajasic, and tamasic. Understanding these categories can help you select foods that are purifying and enjoyable.

- Sattvic foods are pure, inducing calm and meditative feelings. They include milk, honey, whole grains, fruits, nuts, non-root vegetables, and legumes.

- Rajasic foods produce heat, inducing passion and mental hyperactivity. This category includes spicy ingredients such as onions and chili, and stimulants like tea and coffee. Chicken, fish, and root vegetables are also rajasic.

- Tamasic foods induce lethargy and dull the senses, causing negative emotions. These include red meat, alcohol, and mushrooms.

A Tantric diet should be basically sattvic combined with some rajasic foods.

How you prepare and enjoy your food can transform the effect. Prepare and receive the food with gratitude and an open heart. The vibration of the food actually increases. Make your eating time a meditation. Be present—no eating while driving, reading, watching TV, or working on the computer. Celebrate eating. Prepare the setting with devotion, and use simple but beautiful ingredients.

Arrange food attractively. Place fresh flowers on your table and have soothing music playing.

Bless the food. Ask it to work with your body so that which supports the body can be easily assimilated and that which offends the body can be easily eliminated. Enjoy your food by eating slowly. Take pleasure in its aroma, texture, and taste. Allow time to digest your meal properly and to delight in each other's company. Chew food thoroughly to produce enough saliva, which contains essential enzymes, to mix with the food so digestion is quick and complete. When properly chewed, food reaches the stomach in a liquefied state that is easy to digest. If the pieces are too large and digestion too slow, the food especially meat, putrefies and produces toxins, which the body absorbs.

Refrain from drinking liquids with your meals. This encourages washing your food down before it is properly chewed and dilutes the digestive juices, further compromising digestion. This health rule applies even more strongly to iced drinks, which dampen the digestive fire and stop the digestive process. Consume only moderate quantities. Stop eating when you are satisfied, just before you feel full. Finish dinner at least three hours before bedtime.

Let's take a moment to distinguish physical hunger from emotional hunger. Many people turn to food when they are happy and want to celebrate. Some turn to food when

SECRET 4
Prepare the Body Temple

they are unhappy and want comfort. Eating produces endorphins, the body's pleasure hormone. Diets don't work because depriving yourself of that pleasure sets up a backlash as your body rebels and protests.

You still need to eat consciously.

Many people live to eat, rather than eat to live. They primarily choose foods that are familiar and associated with fond childhood memories of love and safety. Some "foodphiles" get defensive when their favorite treats are said to be unhealthy. Every form of psychological protection is employed: denying, invalidating the critic, getting hostile, justifying, etc. How do you react to the inner conflict of loving something that hurts you, or to the threat of losing a major source of comfort or pleasure?

Sugar provides an experience similar to the ecstatic connection, the flow of cosmic energy. It also provides a momentary respite from the pain of spiritual separation. Yet, one teaspoon of that sweet stuff decreases our immune system for up eight hours and for men, it lowers testosterone levels up to 40%.

Sugar is one way we become dehydrated. Almost everyone in the world suffers from chronic dehydration. Virtually every disease that ravages this generation can be linked to dehydration. The body requires at least half a gallon or two litres of pure water every day (more for large people) and even more in hot, dry climates. When thirst prompts you, instead of water, you often turn to coffee or tea. These drinks are diuretics, prompting the body to release water. When we drink fruit juice or soft drinks, the sugar is so toxic that the body must retain a great deal of water to store the sugar in solution and keep it from flooding the bloodstream. That action pulls water out of the system, so there is even less available for proper cell function. For every ounce of these beverages you consume, increase your pure water intake by three ounces.

When water metabolism is askew, calcium ions cannot stay in solution and are deposited in the joints, causing arthritis. Other important ions are eliminated because there isn't enough water to hold them. This causes an oxygen shortage in some cells, making them vulnerable to cancer-causing viruses that thrive in anaerobic (without oxygen) environments. Even five glasses of water a day decreases the risk of colon cancer by 45%, bladder cancer by 50%, and breast cancer by 79%.

Insufficient water is the primary cause of daytime fatigue. Energy shots and drinks only mask the symptoms. Adequate water eases back and joint pain for 80% of sufferers. Just a 2% drop in body water brings on fuzzy minds, short-term memory loss, trouble with basic math, and difficulty focusing on printed material or a computer screen. Even mild dehydration slows the metabolism.

The DNA molecule is in the form of a helix, held together by a water matrix. When there is inadequate water in the cell, the helix collapses and the cell is unable to replicate itself accurately. Therefore, dehydration is a major cause of the cell damage recognized in aging.

You need to be hydrated to move through physical work or exercise. Exercise energizes, fills our cup. Inactivity, on the other hand, increases stiffness and hinders range of motion. Sitting leads to more lethargy, but exercise gets us moving. Your body is designed to move, not sit still for hours on end. Without regular use, muscles atrophy. If you've ever broken a bone and worn a cast, you know how quickly muscle loses its tone when it's not used. Find what you enjoy to get you moving and do it.

Exercise also raises self-esteem and self-image and generates what others perceive as a healthy glow. The more muscle we have, the easier it is to stay slim and trim. Most of us have a desire to be desirable and be seen as attractive.

Exercise can prevent or reverse male erectile dysfunction and help keep the prostate healthy. I know a 58-year -old Olympian bodybuilder who has discovered when he doesn't exercise and do his workout, his libido dips and he has problems with erections. When he gets back to exercising, everything works great. Men's self-esteem and vitality are closely linked to their level of sexual energy and ability to have erections. A man's erections are an indicator of how healthy he really is. When men experience decreased sexual function, often their lives start going on a downward spiral. So get off that couch and get moving. Your woman, prostate, and lingam will love you for it.

Exercise for women can help relieve menstrual cramps and reduce emotional outbursts and stress. Perimenopausal women will get relief from many symptoms, including hot flushes. When women exercise, their testosterone levels rise, reducing the frequency and intensity of hot flushes. It definitely is true for me. When I exercise, even if it's just going for a walk, I hardly get hot flushes. If I miss a day or two, they really get intense.

Dancing, a powerful tool for awakening sexual energy, has always been a part of Tantric ritual. By abandoning yourself ecstatically in dance so that every cell in your body throbs with life, you can transform movement into a transcendental experience. Create an ambience where you can dance without inhibition, alone or with your partner, for up to an hour. Select music that frees and inspires you. Bring your body, heart, and soul into the dance. Let the movements arise out of the sheer joy of expressing yourself physically, emotionally, and spiritually. Good music to dance to includes Gabriel Roth's "Ecstatic Dance," which has the five rhythms. I also like to dance to Enigma's "MCMXCa.D." An hour long, it can become very meditative. I also enjoy belly-dancing. Dissolve into the dance and let it become a celebration of love and life as though you are dancing with the Divine.

How does this apply to lovemaking and sex? We prepare our beautiful body temples before we make love by bathing or showering. Doing it together is more pleasurable because as we can pamper each other. Washing and drying each other and applying lotion, powder, or oil afterward is sensuous. We honor each other. Touch each other with conscious loving touch. Caress and enjoy light pleasure strokes.

I suggest that you trim your pubic hair to be neat and tidy. Some shave. You trim your head hair so why not your pubic hair? Do what makes you feel wonderful, beautiful, sensual, and attractive.

These are just a few ways to prepare your body. It is the only one you get, and there is no replacement. It can regenerate when we give it proper food, water, exercise, and rest.

When you are physically fit, you have the strength to move around and lift your buttocks and pelvis. You can use your knees, legs, and arms to add variety and spice up a lovemaking session. Everyone looks sexier when they are toned. Motion is easier. You feel sexier, no longer embarrassed by jiggling fat. Increased stamina allows for longer lovemaking sessions. You won't get exhausted after a couple of minutes of thrusting. Movement from one position to another is easy. You are more sensitive to the energy moving and have increased sensitivity in your whole body.

In Tantra, there are a series of positions to move from one level to another. If you don't have the mobility or strength, it is not as exciting, stimulating, or enjoyable. If after two minutes of lovemaking you are so winded you can't continue, or your knees give out, or your arms get too tired, that is not fun or enjoyable for either party. Exercise keeps us strong, slim, healthier, and happier, and we tend to live longer. Exercise builds our stamina and heart.

One of my diligent Tantra students now has lovemaking sessions that last for hours and hours. He and his wife love it. As part of his Tantra practice, he eats well and exercises. He has developed greater strength and flexibility, and his erections are stronger and last longer.

In my life, I have been promised long lovemaking sessions. I assumed the man meant all night long or all weekend long, not one or two hours. In my experience, however, I am just getting warmed up when the man is done or too tired to continue.

I purchased a DVD called "Sexual Fitness for Lovers" for couples to get into shape for lovemaking. It can be a fun way to build stamina.

Get into good physical shape and your life and lovemaking

will take on a whole new dimension that has no upper limit. You need the physical strength to go beyond-beyond. Have fun and enjoy!

Sacred Sex, Sacred Life
JANET LEE

"Decorate the walls of the love-chamber beautifully.

Place soft pillows on the bed and liberally sprinkle the sheets with flowers and scent.

Burn sweet incense in the room.

Then let the man and woman ascend to the throne of love."

—Ananga Ranga

SECRET 5

Create a Sacred Space

> FIND PEACE, JOY, AND EQUILIBRIUM
> WITHIN YOUR OWN RELATIONSHIP
> BY GOING CLOSE TO THE SOURCE
> OF CREATION TO PRACTICE
> YOUR TANTRIC MEDITATIONS
> AND LOVE RITUALS.

The sacredness and purity of the environment in which you perform your Tantric rituals supports the creation of your lovemaking area as a space of worship. Tantra teaches us that the external world of objects and events and our internal realm of thoughts and feelings are in a constant interdependent relationship. Through creating a harmonious environment, we can establish for ourselves an inner state of tranquillity and equilibrium.

Create a sanctuary within your home that is dedicated purely for your Tantric rituals. Some of my clients call it the "T-room." First and foremost, your sacred space must be clean, uncluttered, and undisturbed by any outside interference. Arrange the space with your partner, filling it with sensual objects. By using the same space continually, you will eventually build up an energy field and sacred atmosphere within your sanctum.

A shrine should act as a focal point to remind you that your acts are dedicated to love and consciousness. Transform your space with cushions and rugs on the floor. Hang soft materials around your sanctum; include sensual curving shapes to soften hard corners, and adorn plain walls with chiffon, silk, or muslin drapes. To awaken and stimulate the senses and ignite your sexual energy, use Tantric hues of reds, oranges, purples, terra cotta, and saffron. Soft music playing in the background adds to the atmosphere. You will need something soft to lie upon: a bed, rug, mattress, or a massage table.

A shrine needs an altar. It can be simple or as elaborate as you wish. The objects should have special meaning and significance to you. Always dedicate this area by first lighting a candle and/or incense, and/or placing a fragrant flower on your altar and an offering of fresh fruit, if you desire. Honor this sacred space by wearing clothing made of natural fabric, which is comfortable and sensual to the body. I like to wear a soft silk robe.

After a ritual bath, you are ready to enter your sacred space. You can start with conscious breathing and meditating together. Meditation, a major Tantric tool and discipline in the search for enlightenment, instills calmness and focus. It can help you understand yourself while deepening your sense of connection to the cosmic whole. It will teach you to be more in the moment and less in the mind.

A beautiful way to begin and end each meditation or greet one another is with Namaste. Place your hands together in prayer position at your heart. Look into your beloved's eyes and bow slightly. Say "Namaste." That means the divinity within me sees and honors the divinity in you, and you acknowledge the sanctity of the situation.

Assume a comfortable position, sitting in a chair or on the floor with your spine straight yet relaxed. Close your eyes, allowing your thoughts to come and go like clouds floating in the sky. Focus your awareness on your breath. When your attention wanders, bring it back to your breath. Meditate for about 15 minutes per session. (I like to do an open heart meditation.) After meditating, surrender yourselves to the feelings of oneness that fill you with a profound sense of gratitude and grace. Bow down to the earth in a supine posture of prayer. Now you are ready to begin the next phase of worship.

You could now dance or do some yoga positions to ready the body. Once you are in your body and your mind is clear, you can begin to make love with love in your heart towards each other. It is a slow and mystical time.

> "In the right dose, stress is healthy.
>
> Too little stimulation and you are bored; Too much, and you burn out."
>
> —Anonymous

SECRET 6

De-Stress

> "STRESS IS PART OF LIFE. GOOD OR BAD,
> STRESS MAKES US MOVE OR STAY STUCK.
> YOU CAN SEE EVERY SITUATION AS
> A CRISIS OR AN OPPORTUNITY."
>
> —WWW.SECRETSOFTANTRA.COM

One of my clients kept coming for massages, and I kept asking what stresses him out. He replied, "Nothing." I had a hard time believing him. My clairsentience knew that something was brewing, and I told him so. After three massages, he should have been feeling better, but his body was getting worse. I knew he had a high-stress life. I suggested many small lifestyle changes, yet he refused. He was in denial. Then one day, when he was only 32, he had a heart attack. Afterwards, he acknowledged the stressors that filled his life. His choice: make changes or die.

Not all stress is bad. There is both distress (from the Latin dis = bad, as in dissonance, disagreement), and eustress (from the Greek eu = good, as in euphoria). During both eustress and distress, the body undergoes virtually the same responses, yet eustress is considered "healthful or giving one a feeling of fulfillment" (Dictionary.com). A great reminder that it's not just what happens that counts, but how you take it.

Learn to manage stress. Here are twelve easy-to-remember tips on how to bring stress fitness into your life:

Take a break. Get away from it all. Play at something you enjoy. Even a short break will help.

1. Eat healthy foods. Start each day with a healthy breakfast.

2. Talk it out. This is especially true for women. Running over problems in your own mind can make problems seem insurmountable and solutions hard to find. Men tend to retreat into their own mind to figure it out. But there are times when someone else may have a solution for you that you cannot see.

3. Spend time with family and friends. As social beings, we seek companionship and camaraderie to feel connected and have a sense of belonging.

SECRET 6
De-Stress

4. Take a course for fun or self-improvement. Expanding your awareness is the main purpose of life. At every moment, we are either growing (at ease) or dying (*dis-ease*). There are no plateaus.

5. Relax with a good book, massage, a great movie. Be in nature; listen to your favorite music. Get a good night's sleep.

6. Exercise. walk, jog, swim, dance, go to the gym, jump rope, rollerblade, ride a bike—the list is endless. Walk the stairs instead of taking the escalator or elevator. Your body is meant for movement. Exercise stimulates the release of endorphins (feel good hormones) and oxytocin, a natural anti-depressant.

7. Set priorities. Know your values. Get the important things done first. Delegate smaller tasks. Learn to say NO. Before you agree to a task, ask yourself, "Is this moving me forward to my purpose, goals, and vision?"

8. Schedule your time. The hours slip away with frivolous activities. Learn time management skills. Be present with each task until it is completed. Your performance will improve when you are fully present. Be sure to take time to fill your cup.

9. Find internal sources of satisfaction. Start a gratitude journal and be grateful for everything in your life. Become conscious and appreciative. Meditate. Kindness and calm confidence will become a way of being.

10. Start to pay attention to what your body is telling you. Notice your feelings, mood changes, aches and pains, and how you are reacting in situations. When you are clear on your values and in alignment, you feel fulfilled and happy. Notice your "energy zappers"—activities, people, places, things that make you feel tired, stressed, drained, or irritable and what makes you feel enlivened.

11. Take action! Address the person or situation that you find stressful. Don't let things fester. If you're not sure how to manage, talk to a professional. Letting a problem slide in hopes it will go away doesn't work. Which of your needs are not getting met? Do something about it, even if it is only a baby step towards what you want.

In Tantra, we want to experience all life has to offer. There is no side-stepping stress. What matters is how we *deal* with stress. Focus on taking in what you have learned, see the opportunity for growth, and be aware of how fast you get back to center. Does it take a minute, an hour, a day, a month, a year, or never? How far did it throw you off course? How fast can you correct it and get back on track? In the chapter on breathing, I give you a centering exercise to help you get back on track faster.

To be orgasmic with life, we need to experience life in its fullest flavor. Do not back away. Go through whatever you are given, and bliss will infuse your life.

Sacred Sex, Sacred Life
JANET LEE

"Relaxation has miraculous powers.

It will change your behavior outwardly—you will become more calm, more quiet.

It will change the quality of your work—it will be more artistic and more graceful.

You will be committing fewer mistakes than you used to, because now you are more together, more centered....

Relaxation can transform you and transport you to such beautiful heights—and the technique is so simple."

—OSHO

BODY MIND BALANCING:
USING YOUR MIND TO HEAL YOUR BODY.

SECRET 7

Relax

> "OUR BODIES CANNOT HEAL UNTIL WE RELAX.
> ONLY THEN CAN WE HEAL OURSELVES.
> EVEN IN OUR SLEEP, WE ARE NOT RELAXING.
> WE GRIND OUR TEETH, SNORE, TOSS AND TURN,
> WE WAKE UP EXHAUSTED.
> LEARNING HOW TO RELAX AND WHAT IT FEELS LIKE
> CREATES A HAPPIER AND HEALTHIER PERSON.
> MASSAGE IS A GREAT WAY TO FEEL
> YOUR BODY IN A RELAXED STATE."
>
> —WWW.SECRETSOFTANTRA.COM

Do you know what it feels like to be totally relaxed? It is a blissful state that allows energy to flow freely through our bodies to create vitality. Our muscles are toned yet supple. We move with ease, grace, flexibility. We smile more and are happier.

Can you make your body be like a wet noodle? Or is your body like a piece of stiff, uncooked spaghetti? Osho explains relaxation so well in his book, *Tantra, the Supreme Understanding*, that I want to share it with you.

> *What is relaxation? It is a state of affairs where your energy is not moving anywhere, not to the*

> *future, not to the past—it is simply there with you. In the silent pool of your own energy, in the warmth of it, you are enveloped. This moment is all. There is no other moment. Time stops—then there is relaxation. If time is there, there is no relaxation. Simply, the clock stops; there is no time. This moment is all. You don't ask for anything else, you simply enjoy it....*
>
> *Relaxation means this moment is more than enough, more than can be asked and expected. Nothing to ask, more than you can desire—then the energy never moves anywhere. It becomes a placid pool. In your own energy, you dissolve. This moment is relaxation. Relaxation is neither of the body, nor of the mind; relaxation is a total transformation of your energy.*

Relaxation is a state of being. It just feels wonderful to be relaxed. So what are some ways to relax? My favorite is massage. Of course, that is what I do for enjoyment and work. I watch how massage or bodywork transforms people. Afterwards, they look younger, fresher and more alive. Massage is all about touch. To be touched in a loving way can be very relaxing.

Mantak Chia says this about touch:

> *Without regular touch women tend to become depressed and uninterested in sexual touch, while*

CHAPTER 8
Secret 7 - Relax

> *men tend to become more aggressive and become uninterested in touch that is not sexual—a recipe for disharmony.*

Loving, conscious touch is relaxing and healing. Light caresses and strokes soothe the soul.

In my Tantra classes, I teach many different ways to touch. My students are amazed at how touch relaxes the body and mind. They fall into bliss. Men are surprised at how good it feels to be touched slowly, gently, lovingly, and with intent. They marvel at how slow, slow really is. Their amazement increases when they receive positive responses from their partners. One student was so grateful, he cried. He enjoyed it so much, he quit smoking, started eating better, and he smiled more.

The deep pressure of massage not only soothes tired and tense muscles, it also raises levels of serotonin, an antidepressant hormone, by as much as 38% in just 15 minutes, according to studies from the University Of Miami School Of Medicine's Touch Research Institute. "Massage stimulates the vagus nerve, which is involved in releasing serotonin and decreases the stress hormone cortisol," says Institute Director Tiffany Field, PhD. Her prescription: two 20 minute sessions a week. There are so many benefits of massage: enhanced immune system, relaxed muscles, increased sense of well-being and peace, more energy, and the list goes on.

Another relaxation technique is to go out and be in nature. Smell the fresh air and bask in the warmth of the sunshine on your skin. Feel the ground beneath your feet as you walk or run. Sit or lie on the ground. Watch the clouds float by. Hear the birds singing or the water of a brook, creek, river, or sea. Hug a tree if you want. Visit the mountains or the desert. Swim in the ocean or a lake. Nature gets us back in touch with ourselves. Get in touch with nature.

How about a bath or soak in a tub? Add a few drops of a calming essential oil like lavender or jasmine or ylang-ylang. Put on music that soothes your soul. Dim the lights light some candles. I use color baths to revitalize or relax me. Each color has different properties. Shut the world away for a time and just be. Water represents our emotional body. We lived in a "bath" in the womb before we were born. Bathing takes us back to that place of bliss. It calms us. We release all our tension and stress into the water and then let it go down the drain. Water absorbs our fears, tensions, stresses, or whatever is bothering us. We come away feeling relaxed, balanced, and peaceful.

In Tantra, bathing is one of the rituals to slow the mind and cleanse the soul and the body. When you bathe with

Chapter 8
Secret 7 – Relax

your lover, you are preparing each other for lovemaking and seeing the divine in each other. Many people have never experienced bathing with the opposite sex. Bathing is one of the rituals I teach in my Tantra sessions.

Another way to relax is to read a good book. I curl up by the fireplace under a warm blanket in the wintertime or lay out in the sunshine in the summer. Listen to relaxing music. Close your eyes and float with notes and sounds. Listen to the space between the notes. That is how music is created. It is one of the languages of the soul.

Find enjoyable ways to focus on the moment and just be in the moment. It is a great way to take care of yourself and put a smile on your face. Smiling releases oxytocin. It opens the gate above the medulla in the back of the skull that connects us to our spinal column, as well as to the energy tube, known as the sushumna, which is the central system of the subtle body. It makes us relax and release stress and connects us to our hearts. Smiling is healing. Smile and relax your shoulders and body. Enjoy!

Sacred Sex, Sacred Life
JANET LEE

> "Breath is life; and learning to control the breath adds a new dimension of control and ease to every action, no matter how simple or how complex it is.
>
> In fact, the effectiveness of every activity we undertake—singing, walking, working, dancing, public speaking—depends greatly on how we use the air we breathe."
>
> —Nancy Zi
> *The Art of Breathing—Thirty Simple Exercises for Improving Your Performance and Well-Being.*

SECRET 8

Breathe

> "WE ARE A CULTURE OF SHALLOW BREATHERS AND TEND TO HOLD OUR BREATH.
>
> BREATHE DEEP. INHALATION IS "FIRE." HOLDING THE BREATH, WHICH IS CALLED 'AIR', CAUSES MORE HEAT. IF YOU ARE IN PAIN, IT WILL INCREASE THE PAIN.
>
> THE EXHALATION IS 'WATER' AND IS COOLING. A LONG EXHALATION HELPS CLEAR THE MIND.
>
> TO HOLD YOUR BREATH FOR A COUNT OR TWO IS CALLED 'GROUNDING.'
>
> USING EQUAL COUNTS ON ALL STAGES OF BREATH PUTS US IN BALANCE, AND IS CALLED 'ETHER.'"
>
> —WWW.SECRETSOFTANTRA.COM

One very important physiological process we take for granted is breathing. Breathing consciously slows or stops mind chatter and scattered thoughts and keeps us in the present moment.

I am going to explain several simple but profound breathing methods. The first one is used in Tantra yoga. It is called four-sided breathing.[10]

---

10. Shawn Roop. TantraQuest.com, 2005.

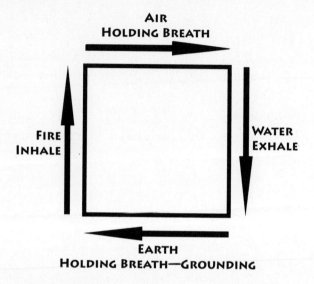

Inhalation relates to the "fire" element. It provides the energy to get things moving. Its key component is oxygen. We can use fire to create stress, excitement, or tension.

Holding the breath at the top parallels the "air" element. Add air to fire and you get more fire. Therefore, we can create more pain, more tension, more excitement (especially in sex), or more stress. There is also the component of meditative breathing when the breath naturally stops for a period when the mind is still. This is healthy and should not cause concern. Breath naturally resumes on its own when you need it.

Secret 8
Breathe

Exhalation relates to the "water" element. Notice that when you breathe out onto your hand, it is moist. Water represents our emotions. Our bodies are mostly water. Exhaling releases stress, tension, and pain, reduces the excitement level somewhat, and brings us back to center.

Grounding is the "earth" element. Holding our breath for a moment after exhalation grounds us back to earth.

If you want balance in your life, you breathe in "ether" or "prana," which connects body, mind, and spirit. You accomplish this by breathing equally on all four sides. An example: Inhale for 3 seconds. Hold your breath for 3 seconds. Exhale for 3 seconds. Hold the emptiness for 3 seconds.

You can use many combinations for breathing consciously. If you are stressed or emotional and need to calm down or reduce pain, breathe out longer than the other sides. If you need more energy, breathe in longer and hold the inhalation for a few seconds before a quick out breath.

One pregnant client was so stressed out about having to deliver her fourth child that I taught her this breathing technique. She used it for every stressful situation up to and through the delivery. She was calm and everything went very well.

The second breathing method is for centering. It is called the "Pharaoh's breath." It is a cycle of 3 breaths. You can do all the steps anywhere or at anytime, except when you are driving. In that case, do only steps 2 through 7.

1. Close your eyes (but not while you are driving).

2. Take a long, slow exhalation through the mouth.

3. Follow this with a normal inhalation through the nose.

4. Take another long, slow exhalation through the mouth.

5. Follow with another normal inhalation through the nose.

6. Take a third long, slow exhalation through the mouth.

7. Follow with a third normal inhalation through the nose.

8. Resume normal breathing. Say to yourself, "Centering exercise for 10 seconds."

9. Picture or imagine a circle and a dot.

10. Notice where your dot is.

11. Take a long, slow exhalation through the mouth.

12. Open your eyes.

Secret 8

Breathe

The dot represents you. The circle is your life. Where are you in the circle? Are you even in the circle? When you see the dot in the center of the circle, you are centered. Do this when you feel scattered or need clarity of mind, grounding, or to de-stress. Use Steps 2 through 7 without the visualization to calm down and create a sense of well-being.

I have taught this to most of my clients, and it works. One woman, who was stressed almost to the point of burn out, couldn't believe that breathing would do anything for her. It was too simple. In her early attempts, she was not in the circle. She couldn't even see a circle. After a little practice, she saw the circle and then the dot. On the last cycle of breathing, she was in the center of the circle. This took all of about three minutes. When we finished, she was calm, relaxed, and her whole body felt light. She decided at that time to make some key changes in her situation when before she couldn't see any solutions. Her whole life transformed into one of greater harmony. Many of my clients use this and are very grateful to know something so simple can be so transformative.

Hawaiians call North Americans "howlies," which means "shallow breathers." Shallow breathing gets very little oxygen into the system, increasing stress and inhibiting fat utilization. While it's tempting to disengage from the body and become numb to emotions and pain rather than deal with life's stresses, it is important to listen to your body's signals and take affirmative action to support the body's attempts center itself. Deep breathing into the belly and down to the pelvic floor muscles relaxes the body, enabling you to feel more and become more conscious of your body and your surroundings.

I use breath work in my massage and Tantra sessions. Deep breathing helps to relax the body and mind. It releases tight muscles, lets endorphins flow, and slows runaway thoughts. In Tantra, deep breathing, cycle breathing, and rapid breathing are used in different ways for ejaculation mastery and/or full body orgasms.

For men, deep, slow breathing into the belly or into the PC muscle[11] followed by squeezing the PC muscle slows down the dopamine hormone surge and releases oxytocin, the bonding hormone instead. This helps delay ejaculation, prolongs pleasure, and creates a sense of peace, all the while building up energy to be used in many ways—healing, youthfulness and vitality, manifestation, building wealth, increased self-confidence, spirituality, connection.

---

11. The pubococcygeous, or PC muscle, is a group of important pelvic floor muscles that run from your pubic bone (pubo) in the front, to your tailbone or coccyx (coccygenus) in the back.

Secret 8
Breathe

Cycle breathing is used in Tantra. After learning how to breathe deeply and relax, the next step is to move the energy, including sexual energy. Inhale deeply into the perineum and squeeze the PC muscle. On the exhale, relax or release the PC muscle, move the energy and breath up the spine, over the top of your head, back down to the roof of your mouth. Now touch your tongue to the roof of your mouth just behind your front teeth. This is your sexual meridian. Repeat the cycle again as many times as you like or until you reach an orgasmic state. This creates bliss and heightened levels of pleasure.

Cycle breathing is very useful at the moment of orgasm. Use the breath to move your energy up the spine to your heart center, and then send the energy up out of your heart center and over the top of your head, back into the heart center in the front. This path mirrors the *ankh*, the symbol of immortality, and you retain all the energy from the orgasm instead of giving it away. (The ankh, pictured here, is the cross with the round circle on the top)

THE ANCIENT ANKH, SYMBOL OF LIFE

My was-band (ex-husband) was afraid to try this breath. I did it all the time, and I looked years younger than he. Some of my clients who do this can create multiple orgasms for themselves. It takes a lot of focus at first, yet it is so worth the effort. They all report their lovemaking just keeps getting better. Some have reported they feel like they are 16 again.

"Fire orgasmic" breathing is rapid breathing to increase the fire in the belly. It heightens sexual energy, and body temperature will rise. This type of breathing is great for people with low libido, poor erections, men who have problems ejaculating, and for anorgasmic[12] women. Non-sexually, fire breathing is great when you feel very cold or when you are extremely tired and need a boost of energy. This breath facilitates body orgasms (whole body involved, not just genitals). It is enjoyable, not dependent on the presence of a partner, and can be done anywhere at any time.

The basic practice is:

1. Take a sharp breath (sort of like a "snort") through your nose, fast, deep, and rapid.

2. Exhale quickly through the mouth, saying "Hah!"

3. No holding the breath. Be careful not to hyperventilate, or you will get light-headed.

---

12. Anorgasmic: the inability to achieve sexual orgasms

4. Move your energy through your body and energy centers until you fill your body (your container) with sexual energy and fire.

5. When done properly, you have orgasms. Your cells vibrate at a higher frequency for hours afterward, and you are energized.

6. Enjoy!

One female student from my orgasm workshop started doing this breath work. She had never had an orgasm before. It took some practice, but we got her to a heightened energetic state. When she went home and started to do the breathing pattern, the next day she had multiple orgasms. Her persistence paid off, and she is one happy woman.

Goddess breath is an exchange of a breath with a partner. The breath can be either simultaneous or alternating on the inhalation and exhalation. It can get quite intoxicating, especially when sitting in yab-yum[13] position.

Simultaneous breathing—both persons breathe in and out at the same time and in sync with each other. This is the best exercise to start and end your sessions as well as anything you do together. Nose to nose works nicely. This can be intoxicating, too.

---

13. Yab-yum is the ultimate Tantra position. You sit cross-legged, facing the other partner's lap with the lighter partner sitting on the top of the partners lap. You can unite genitals if you wish.

Sacred Sex, Sacred Life
JANET LEE

In the alternating breath, done through the mouth or nose, the out-breath or exhale becomes the lingam, and the in-breath or inhale becomes the yoni. One person exhales into the mouth or nose of the other person while they are inhaling, taking the breath and energy all the way down into the belly. Each squeezes their PC muscle (for more stimulation and excitement), then moves the energy up the spine for the exhale (as the other person is inhaling) and moves the energy down to the PC and/or genitals on the inhale, continuing to go back and forth until you get tired or need to stop. Body and heart orgasms are common with this practice.

Most of my clients really love this breath and cannot believe how erotic and energizing it is. They quickly experience a heightened state sexually and sensually. The more they practice it, the more they want to do it. They are now hooked on Tantra.

One of my clients has become addicted to this practice. We breathe together and all time stops; the connection is indescribable. We become one with the divine. His life has become more enjoyable and his work less stressful. He responds to situations instead of reacts. His employees love him for this. They have no idea what has come over their boss, but they are grateful.

Secret 8
Breathe

Breath work is important in all areas of life. If we are unaware of our breath, we are probably unaware in our lives. Breath helps keeps us in our body and in the present moment.

There is one last breath I have been practicing. I do this while I practice my self-healing. It is called "consciousness breathing." This is how we connect to the universe. There are no pauses between inhalation and exhalation. It is one continuous breath in and out, like the waves on the ocean. To do this, slowly breathe deep into your stomach to relax the body and calm the mind. Then exhale with the same measured slowness to release all stress and tension. Continue to breathe this way for up to 20 minutes. Your intuition will become sharp; you will develop a sense of calm, confidence, and the behaviors you don't like will change automatically. It is truly magical. If you do this for a few minutes at night before sleep and when you wake in the morning, you stay connected to the divine, and life flows more easily.

To feel all the wonderful sensations life has to offer, breathe and breathe deeply. Take in a complete breath. Feel it going into your belly and expanding into your back and sides. It should move your whole torso. Watch a newborn breathe. They know how, but we have forgotten. Become childlike in your breathing. Enjoy and become peaceful.

Sacred Sex, Sacred Life
JANET LEE

"The Love Muscle"

The pubococcygeous, or PC, muscle is known in Tantra as the 'love muscle,' and exercising and toning it greatly enhances the creation and control of sexual energy.

Awareness of your love muscle helps you to feel more in touch with your body, genital area, and sexual response.

—MICHELLE PAULI

SEX WITH SPIRIT.

SECRET 9

Squeeze the Love Muscle

> THE PUBOCOCCYGEOUS OR PC MUSCLE MUST BE DEVELOPED FOR YOU TO BECOME MULTI-ORGASMIC. TO LEARN TO ISOLATE THESE MUSCLES, BOTH MEN AND WOMEN, CAN START AND STOP THE FLOW WHILE URINATING. ONCE YOU GET THE IDEA, YOU CAN PRACTICE SQUEEZING AT ANY TIME; THEN SEE WHAT HAPPENS WHEN YOU SQUEEZE DURING LOVEMAKING.
>
> THE NEXT STEP IS TO PRACTICE SQUEEZING YOUR ANUS MUSCLE. THIS IS ESPECIALLY IMPORTANT FOR MEN, AS THIS WILL STIMULATE AND MASSAGE THE PROSTATE GLAND TO KEEP IT HEALTHY AND TO PREVENT IT FROM BECOMING SWOLLEN OR ENLARGED.
>
> —WWW.SECRETSOFTANTRA.COM

The muscles in the pelvic floor hold all the organs of the lower abdomen in place. This "sling" is vital to your health and sexual life. Ask anyone with bladder problems (incontinence), uterus problems (fibroids, endometriosis, prolapsed uterus), or bowel problems—it is NOT FUN. It disrupts your work life, playtime, sex life, and your sleep.

I have many clients with some of the above problems. Men don't want to admit they are incontinent. Women quietly take antibiotics for bladder infections. The problems are so easy to solve if they would *just squeeze that muscle.*

I have two clients, in particular, who both have to rush to the washroom constantly. Golfing or going on an airplane is quite embarrassing at times. One chose to ignore the problem until it became out of control. Now he goes to physical therapy, only to be told to squeeze the PC muscle and have anal massage. I had encouraged him for several years to do just that.

Another male client had to go for treatments. They inserted a catheter through the penis to the bladder and used an IV drip to insert the antibiotics. This procedure was uncomfortable, embarrassing, and didn't work well. So they tried a laser treatment to cut away some prostate tissue. That didn't work either, so he is back to the IV treatments. If you want to end up in the same situation or something similar, don't squeeze that PC muscle. He is not willing to put the effort in to see if it will improve his situation. Too bad! Squeezing the PC muscle is so simple. No one knows you are doing it. When you urinate, start and stop the flow several times. I do this every time I go to the washroom. I have strong muscles. My bladder is very healthy.

Another way for men to maintain a strong PC muscle is to bob your lingam or penis. You did that as a boy or when

SECRET 9
Squeeze the Love Muscle

you wanted to show off your erections. My "was-band" loved to do this. We called these penis push-ups. You can add a facecloth on an erect penis and bob it up and down. Once you get stronger, use a wet one. Then increase the weight with a hand towel, bath towel, and finally a sheet.

The Taoists are very adamant that one should have strong PC muscles. Women are encouraged to practice holding benwa balls in the vagina to make it strong and keep the female organs healthy. Women, try using these "vagina barbells." They build up the muscles very fast.

Have you ever made love just squeezing your PC muscles? The sensations are more subtle but oh, so yummy! Being able to move the muscles during intercourse creates an energy that engages the whole body, creating more heart and body orgasms.

Once you know where the PC muscles are, you can add the anus muscle as well. No abdominal or leg muscles allowed. This increases the sensations and blood flow. For men, as mentioned earlier, this exercise will massage and "milk" the prostate gland to keep it healthy and prevent prostate enlargement.

Now you can add breath work and squeezing to move more energy around. One way is to exhale all the air from your abdomen and lungs and squeeze the abdominals towards the spine and the PC muscle toward your lower abdomen. Hold until you can't hold it any longer. Breathe in, releasing all the tension and allowing the air to rush into the belly. This is the beginning of ecstatic breath work. It relaxes the first and second chakras[14] (genital and lower abdominal regions) to create an orgasmic response instead of a trauma response.

In trauma response, we tense everything up and hold our breath, stopping the flow of blissful energy. Orgasmic response is relaxed and creates the body sensations necessary for multiple orgasms. The pelvis moves freely in a pelvic tilt/release motion, creating, instead of the normal tension, a relaxed motion that frees the pelvis and increases energy movement. Add deep breathing and gentle pelvic rocking, and you will create blissful and peaceful orgasms that last for a very long time.

Toning the pelvic floor muscles will strengthen your lower abdominals and low back and improve bladder control (for both genders). You have now started some core stability strength training and set the foundation for extraordinary sex.

For women, the stronger the PC muscles, the better toned you become. The more toned the vagina and uterus,

14. Chakras are spinning energy wheels along the sushumna, or central channel of the subtle body.

SECRET 9
Squeeze the Love Muscle

the stronger you will be overall. You will have fewer problems with your menstrual cycle because the toning minimizes mood swings and blood flow. Your attitude about being female will be more positive as this helps you step into the empowerment of the Goddess.

For men, the stronger your PC muscle, the healthier your prostate will be. You will have stronger and longer-lasting erections. Your overall self-esteem and confidence will increase, and your lovemaking will take on new meaning and enjoyment.

Please squeeze that PC muscle and see how it can change your life, especially your sex life.

Sacred Sex, Sacred Life
JANET LEE

> "...the emphasis of our work is on producing better orgasms for women.
>
> We feel that the best lover is the one who can produce the most pleasure.
>
> To become an artist in 'doing' makes a man an extremely valuable commodity."
>
> —STEVE AND VERA BODANSKY, PHD'S
> *EXTENDED MASSIVE ORGASM*

SECRET 10

Men are to Serve Women

"THIS DOES NOT MEAN MEN ARE TO BE SLAVES TO WOMEN. IT MEANS MEN ARE THERE TO PLEASURE WOMEN TO THE FULL NINE LEVELS OF ORGASM. ONCE SHE REACHES THAT LEVEL, SHE WILL SURRENDER TO YOU ALL THE NAGGING, COMPLAINING, WHINING, ETC. WILL COME TO A HALT, AND YOU WILL BE A VERY HAPPY MAN."

—WWW.SECRETSOFTANTRA.COM

Wow!

What a statement? When a man opens his heart to a woman, he is making love to her. And when they connect eye-to-eye, genital-to-genital, heart-to-heart, soul-to-soul, there is "no-thing" like this state. You become orgasmic with the universe, blending together until the two are truly one in every sense—simple, not easy, but very simple.

The lingam (penis), the "God wand of love" or "wand of light" is to worship the yoni—the female genitalia known as the "sacred garden", the "sacred alter" or the "sacred gateway". Only women can carry a child and give birth. Only women bleed. Women are blessed with this awesome and powerful gift. When a man uses his lingam with the intention of love and penetrates with love, it is the most beautiful and wonderful experience. There is nothing like it.

Men have been very afraid of women's sexual energy and orgasms over the centuries and have perpetuated this fear. Men taught women to only satisfy the male ejaculation and ego. Women have been left out and not loved to their fullest expression of being a woman.

Men need to be present and listen to what a woman is saying. Hold back the urge to be the "knight in shining armor." You are there to listen. Hold the energy or space while she is explaining what is going on in her life, then you may ask if she needs any help or assistance. Most of the time, a woman just needs to get her thoughts out of her head, and she usually will find her own solution. She will be grateful to you for your undivided attention and for supporting her process.

My partner learned this the hard way while we taking our Tantra training. We were practicing the fire orgasmic breathing, and I went into a high state of vibration and energy. He thought I was in distress, and he wanted to comfort and

SECRET 10
Men are to Serve Women

rescue me. I didn't want him near me. The teacher was there and instructed him to leave me alone and leave the room. After I came back to earth, he was allowed to re-enter the room and space. He was told he needs to learn to hold the space and just be there—no rescuing and rushing in to "fix it." Nothing was broken. It was being transformed into a new form and needed the room to grow and change.

In one of our Open Heart Meditation evenings, there were two women and three men present. We finished our meditation, and the other woman was put into the center of our circle for a healing for her and her son who had been hospitalized that day. She became overwhelmed and started to cry. We just let her process. I then went to her to hold her with an open loving heart while the men held space for us. No one rescued her. We were just there to honor her and allow her to feel loved. Afterward, she gratefully thanked us and especially the men for "being" there to keep the love energy flowing. It was beautiful—a true Tantra experience. Two of the men really didn't "know" what to do but their intuition told them what needed to be done—send love and hold the space. Now they understand how they can serve women better.

To help men learn to serve women, it would be helpful to know that men and women have completely different types of orgasms. In Dr. Stephan T. Chang's book, the *Tao of Sexology, the Book of Infinite Wisdom*,[15] it is stated:

> *Different orgasms are the direct and indirect causes of much of humanity's pain...Acquisition of knowledge is the first step toward understanding male and female orgasms...*
>
> *To facilitate the study of female orgasms, the female orgasm has been separated into nine steps or stages of experience. These nine steps are joined together and overlap in various degrees, creating multi-level experiences.*
>
> *A woman in orgasm can be described as a blooming lotus flower. A woman experiencing a complete orgasm...undergoes nine stages of blossoming until she finally opens up and surrenders herself to the man who has served her.*

These nine levels may seem small and insignificant, but they are important to watch for in ourselves as women and for men to become familiar with, as they are predictable. These observations were made centuries ago by the Taoists, and in my experience they are absolutely accurate. As each level of orgasm is reached, different organs are energized. Each level may not seem like the "big O," yet it is an orgasmic response.

15. Dr. Stephen T. Chang, *Tao of Sexology: The Book of Infinite Wisdom* (Reno, NV: Tao Publishing, 1986) 96-97.

SECRET 10
Maen are to Serve Women

The first level engages the lungs, as the woman sighs and breathes heavily. She will start to salivate. The second level moves to the heart. As she is kissing you, she will offer her tongue to you, and the tongue corresponds to the heart. (Hence, French kissing is one of the tantra kisses.) On the third level, the organs involved are the spleen, pancreas and stomach. Her muscles become activated, and she will grasp for you and hold you tight.

The fourth level is the key. Most of the time, this is where the action stops, and it can cause the women many problems in her kidneys and bladder. Vaginal spasms occur, and the secretions start to flow. Many men think this is the orgasm she is seeking, and it is not. He can take her to the higher levels with just a little movement.

Next her joints begin to loosen, and she might start to bite. Then, on level six, the woman undulates and gyrates wrapping her legs around the man. The liver and nerves are now energized. Level seven "boils" the blood, and she is trying to grasp the man everywhere. The muscles are now involved and totally relaxed in level eight. She may grab the man's nipples and bite even more.

Orgasm has come on this final level. The whole body is energized, and she will totally surrender and open up. Her whole being is ready to be loved totally and completely.

This is why ejaculation mastery is very important. When she reaches the ninth level, she can surround you both with incredible passion and love, leaving you both fulfilled and satisfied.

If a woman is having trouble with certain organs, it could be a sign of an imbalance caused by never having achieved the corresponding orgasmic level in lovemaking. Again, it is important to be aware and observe what is happening in the body. Both of you will be healthier and happier.

Osho, a Tantric master, viewed things a bit differently. Here is what he has to say to men: in the book *Sex Matters—From Sex to Superconsciousness*:

> *Help her come out of her castle. She lives in a castle, so bring her out. Love her more. She will only understand the language of love. And three things for you:*
>
> *One: love her more but don't ask for sex. If she invites you, only then, otherwise not...because your very effort will create a resistance in her. So simply love, be loving; be prayerful, but don't ask for sex...*
>
> *Never force sex on any woman, and you will be surprised; they will be running around you wagging their tails, because they need it as much as you. They love it as much as you—in fact more than you, because a woman can enjoy sex more than a man. For a man, sex is a very local affair. For a woman it*

SECRET 10
Men are to Serve Women

is a very big thing, bigger than herself. Man is a big circle and sex is a small circle within it. The woman is just the opposite: sex is a big circle and the woman is a small circle within it.

And the second thing: she has a very anti-attitude about the body, so don't touch her body with any lust in your mind. When you feel lustful don't touch her body... When you are lustful, you are asking for sex, you are starved. Then the whole mind is just planning for sex... When you are feeling very happy and contented and there is no need for any other's body, then touch her body in a very prayerful mood, and she will be very happy. She will be able to see that you are not asking for the body. That is the way you can help her to come out of her condemnatory, anti-body attitude.

And the third thing: don't be together too much. That's how many love affairs are destroyed. Enjoy your own space alone and let her also enjoy her space alone. Sometimes meet, sit together, but don't make it a twenty-four hour affair. Leave her alone so that she starts having some appetite for you, otherwise the appetite is killed...the more you are missing, the more she misses you. Then, when you come, she will be more open to receive you. So first create the appetite, then you can enjoy the meal.

I agree with Osho on these three things men can do for women. I can sense the moment a man is lustful. He may not know it, but I do. His actions and touch are totally different than when a man demonstrates love and relates from his heart. I have talked with other women, and most have the same awareness.

One woman client tells me she only wants lust. She loves lustful and raunchy sex. Then in the next breath, she doesn't understand why she can't get into a loving and long-lasting relationship. Men get tired of lustful sex too.

A lot of my male clients are on anti-depressants or have anxiety issues. They are also craving the intimacy of a loving relationship. They have become uninterested in sex or they have developed performance anxiety. Their wives are either uninterested in anything to do with them, or the men have developed premature ejaculation problems.

Men do truly want to please and give pleasure to a woman. They need to be guided and know what women want. Women need to know what they want and not be afraid to speak up. The more women are honored and the more women honor themselves, the better our relationships will become.

Both Osho and Chang suggest ways men can bring their partners to new levels of pleasure and not fear her wonderful, powerful energy. So, all you loving men open your heart and let her fall in. You will both be happy and healthy. Life will be even more wonderful.

> "Becoming multi-orgasmic, like becoming a skilful lover, requires that you discover and learn to master your own arousal."
>
> —MATAK CHIA
> *THE MULTI-ORGASMIC COUPLE.*

SECRET 11

The Masculine Principle – Ejaculation Mastery

> "LEARN THE DIFFERENCE BETWEEN ORGASM AND EJACULATION. EVERY TIME A MAN EJACULATES, HE LOSES LIFE-FORCE ENERGY THAT COULD BE USED FOR REGENERATION, HEALING, RE-ENERGIZING. HAVING MULTIPLE ORGASMS WITHOUT EJACULATING CAN PLEASE BOTH PARTNERS INTO BLISS."
>
> —WWW.SECRETSOFTANTRA.COM

When the man takes the dominant role in lovemaking, he is able to experience his strength and assertiveness in the sexual situation. This can be a powerful aphrodisiac for both sexes. At the same time, however, he should remain aware and sensitive to the needs of his partner and be conscious of her pleasure. By allowing this combination of tenderness and power to occur, the man is realizing his masculine potential: the active "solar" aspect that complements perfectly the passive "lunar" aspect of the woman's femininity.

Men are fire energy, quick to ignite and quick to extinguish. Women are water energy, slower to bring to a boil and steam. Men need to cool their fire to bring the woman to her nine levels of orgasm. Women usually need a lot of time.

Try to avoid overexcitement, which propels you toward an early release, especially if your partner has not yet attained her orgasmic threshold. Take the pressure out of the situation by stopping or slowing activity well before you reach the "point of no return." Breathe slowly and deeply into your abdomen, and relax the muscles surrounding your genitals and anus.

Can a man really have multiple orgasms without ejaculation? The answer is a resounding yes! From the Tantric perspective, orgasm is not a goal or completion of sex, but rather an aroused physical and emotional state that literally can be experienced throughout one's entire being. The longer you linger in this aroused state of excitement, the more energy and life-force you can absorb and radiate. A man may have multiple orgasms without ejaculation and actually feel energized in the afterglow. It can be extraordinarily satisfying to be with a man who can continue to ride wave upon wave of pleasure. It creates a deep and profound feeling of union.

SECRET 11
The Masculine Principal – Ejaculation Mastery

The techniques that assist one in developing these skills can be learned and mastered with practice. During ejaculation, an immense amount of proteins, vitamins, minerals, and amino acids, as well as vital energies from all his organs, are lost in the ejaculate (as it is to be used to create a new life). This depletion doesn't mean that a man should never ejaculate, but rather should do so with consciousness and wisdom. When a man ejaculates this way—and if he plants his seed along with an intentional thought or vision—it becomes a conscious conception, whether it's for a baby or an empowering state that one can conjure and imprint. It is infused with the creative life force or feminine energy.

A non-ejaculatory type of orgasm for a man can occur repeatedly without leaving him exhausted. Once a man ejaculates and "spills his seed," he is usually tired and ready to go to sleep. This is because prolactin, a depressant hormone, has been released. If he is older than 35, his testosterone hormone level is already on the decline. Tantric practices offer him the ability to maintain a level of heightened arousal with numerous peaks and multiple dimensions of exhilarating pleasure, and many men find this to be more satisfying.

The key is to be able to be excited or stimulated and relaxed at the same time. On the pleasure scale of 1 to 10, a man can learn to maintain a level of 7 (which is heaven) or higher for as long as he desires. Breathing and movement exercises can assist one in opening up to feeling fabulously aroused while calm and centered at the same time. Orgasms are deep like the ocean. A man can learn to ride the waves and experience great pleasure and the immense benefits that it brings.

Depending on a man's health, his age, and other factors, frequent ejaculation can be depleting. With Tantric techniques, he can learn to actually re-absorb his vital essences and become empowered by them. When a man doesn't ejaculate during orgasm, he is able to effectively move the energy and fill his body with a highly charged and oxygenated life force. Through simple techniques, a man can reach an orgasmic state that satisfies on a deep and peaceful level. In fact, men who don't ejaculate after sustaining high levels of pleasure often feel energized and rejuvenated afterwards. This expanded state can last for days and can lead to a highly refined sensitivity to pleasure. This profound experience can be enjoyed solo or with a partner. With proper guidance and practice, men often find a Tantric orgasm more pleasurable and satisfying than an orgasm with release.

When a man has multiple orgasms, he awakens him to an experience very similar to that of a woman's sensation.

SECRET 11

The Masculine Principal – Ejaculation Mastery

Men often report feelings of pleasure that rise to their heart with a lightness and glowing warmth that radiates throughout the body. Men who are multi-orgasmic have the potential to become more emotionally intimate and able to join with a woman in conscious sexual bliss. When a man discovers his ability to relax into pleasure, he rises to a new level that can only be understood through direct experience. Relaxing into pleasure is a gateway that can open him up to realizing his full spectrum of orgasmic states.

Are you man enough to do something totally different and change your mindset? When you self-pleasure or self-love, you can practice this technique. Begin by breathing into your PC muscle and squeeze the muscle while stroking and loving your lingam. You might need a lubricant. When you get to a level 7 or 8 state of arousal, hold your breath and squeeze your PC muscle and hold both for about 20 seconds. This is called the "big draw." Relax, and let the energy move around your body. Start the process again. Each time you peak to level 7 or 8, do the big draw, and then drop your energy back down to about a level 5. Do this a few times. Don't be surprised if you go from a level 5 to level 10 in a few moments and ejaculate, as it will take you by surprise. These peaks and valleys create the oxytocin wave.

Once you master this, try to hold yourself at a level 9 or 9.5 to do some peaking and dropping. Remember to relax and breathe. This is very important. After awhile, the desire to ejaculate will disappear, and you'll feel on top of the world. Eventually, you become able to jump the level 10 and go beyond-beyond as there is no upper limit. You won't have the desire to ejaculate unless you want to and are conscious of the reason to do so.

I have a hard time expressing this to men. Those who are willing to reach this state of euphoria and become infused with incredible energy and start to become consciously aware can experience full-body orgasms lasting anywhere from a few minutes to half an hour or more. Some men even begin to levitate. Their legs and arms start to float off the table. Some men see vivid colors. On occasion, their whole bodies vibrate– their fingers and toes tingling. Every cell is alert and vibrating at a higher frequency. When this occurs, they are hooked!

They find out their pleasure is way beyond their wildest imagination, a pleasure greater than ejaculating. They are more confident, stand taller, feel younger, and their increased energy levels can last for days or weeks.

I have one client whose energy remains elevated for over a month. He doesn't get sick anymore, has no muscle soreness, is smiling, and has energy to burn. He is also over sixty years old.

SECRET 11
The Masculine Principal – Ejaculation Mastery

Another client experiences a constant state of orgasmic energy and is not interested in the goal of ejaculating anymore. He can now breathe and squeeze his PC muscle, and in just in a few moments, he is having full body orgasms.

For one client, the back and sciatic pain that plagued him for over 20 years has disappeared.

I do hope you will consider this an alternative way of being and see a new, stronger man emerge. And in the process, I hope you become a wonderful lover.

Sacred Sex, Sacred Life
JANET LEE

> "...a woman doesn't have enlightenment; she thinks she does.
>
> A woman is already enlightened when she is in a state of love such that... she has realized or seen God in man.
>
> And she has that consciousness that is just woman—which is to say, pure love."
>
> —BARRY LONG,
> AUTHOR OF
> *MAKE LOVE THE DIVINE WAY*

SECRET 12

The Feminine Principle – Doorway to Enlightenment

> "WOMEN ARE TO COMPLETELY LOVE A MAN WITH AN OPEN HEART. IN SUCH A STATE, SHE TEACHES A MAN HOW TO LOVE WITH AN OPEN HEART AND SHE WILL RECEIVE THE NURTURING SHE DESIRES AND NEEDS."
>
> —WWW.SECRETSOFTANTRA.COM

A woman's sexual fulfillment is of paramount importance to Tantra. She is equal in all things and, indeed, is regarded as the initiator and kinetic force of sexual energy. According to Tantra, no man can be sexually satisfied unless his woman is filled with joy and love from the union. It is important to give the female partner the freedom to express herself sexually both in the active and passive positions. In addition, switching roles allows the man to surrender himself to her erotic feminine power.

So, what comes first? Do we teach women to open their hearts to teach men to love them, or do we teach men to open their hearts to love women more? My partner and I have long discussions about this. Who teaches whom and how do men and women respond openly and lovingly to each other? We also laugh a lot. There are times when we are figuring it out and then, when we reach a new level of awareness, we start again at the beginning.

Enlightenment is simply rising above a limited self-concept, returning to that basic unity that has always been, and realizing the light within. Enlightenment is a return to the Source that created you, an awareness of the Source of your energy, and a oneness with that Source.

Women seem to come by this naturally. Most of us relate to the world through the feminine essence, or energy. Feminine energy is nurturing, communicative, intuitive, and relationship-oriented. We feel and express unconditional love, especially with our children. Love is the essence from which all is created, and we carry love in our hearts. Women want to be loved completely. In this way, they are directly connected to Source.

Biologically, the female brain is designed to promote nesting, nurturing, and to protect the immediate surroundings. Women have better peripheral vision than men.

SECRET 12
The Feminine Principle – Doorway to Enlightenment

They are wired to communicate verbally, and relationships are of the utmost importance.

At the spiritual retreats I attend, the women are the ones having orgasms all day long when they connect with Source's love. They are so in tune with that vibration, it is wonderful to witness.

The masculine energy is proactive, protective, and more analytical than intuitive. It can be challenging for a man to access an "open heart full of love" experience. One approach I have found quite successful is to have the man lay face down, and I lie on his back and ask him to allow me to fall into his heart. When I feel his heart, even slightly, he can feel our hearts beating together and in sync. Then he rolls over onto his back, and I lay face-to-face with him. We start a conscious breathing process and connect that way. Once we feel the flow of energy, I ask again to let me fall into him. When he can, we go deeper and deeper. The heart opens more, and if we are very connected in our hearts, we have heart orgasms. The man is so moved by this and how his heart feels, he changes and starts to understand what I have been talking about. Once he experiences it, it means something to him.

Diane Richardson from *Tantric Orgasm for Women* says:
Women are afraid to talk to men about sex and are reluctant to share with men what pleases our bodies

> *most. The main fear for a woman is that of losing her man, of ceasing to be sexually attractive to him if she changes. Sadly, when we women choose to stay with conventional sex—which are distorted forms of male sexuality—we give away our unique feminine magic and power.*

In the active sexual role, a women can consciously develop the art of receiving and channelling masculine sexual energy upward during intercourse and can lift sex to another dimension for herself and her man. She can guide her man into an expanded sexual sphere, and thereby create for herself more satisfying sexual experiences. A feminine essence woman has the natural capacity to enter this realm. She, as the receptive aspect in the male/female dynamic, can move inward and draw or pull her man along with her. This is her intrinsic power. Through receptivity, through giving way and yielding, inherent movement is possible. The opposite does not necessarily hold true: generally speaking, a man cannot easily initiate the experience of opening a doorway and absorbing woman into him. To do so requires great stillness and the clarity of true male authority. When the receptive (feminine) aspect gives way, actually receiving, it's this very receptivity that enables the dynamic (masculine) energy to move and flow. In this way, the man easily and naturally follows the woman; he can even wordlessly flow into exalted realms

SECRET 12
The Feminine Principle – Doorway to Enlightenment

with the woman, if he is fortunate enough to encounter receptive feminine energy.

Therefore, the woman is the real starting point for the necessary sex re-education. This movement must first take root in women to spread out into society. It requires that women begin to speak up, express their needs and sensitivities, and for men to take urgent heed of these messages. The greatest potential for true sexual fulfillment and love lies in a woman and a man joined together on a mutual journey of sexual self-discovery.

The secret of Tantra sex lies in bringing that which is sexually unconscious into full consciousness. Osho says, "Tantra is the transformation of sex into love through awareness." This illustrates the point that how we do something is infinitely more important that what we do.

When women are willing to step up and teach their man with love, respect, and patience by speaking from their hearts, men are more likely to respond with open hearts. When men are trustable, willing to stand steady with heart open and share the space of love for a woman with respect and good listening skills, women are free to surrender into bliss to create bliss for both.

We have both the feminine and masculine energies within each of us. That makes us each whole and complete. We cannot have one without the other. They complement each other.

I like to use the analogy of the river and river bank. The river bank is the masculine aspect; it gives direction and structure for the water. The river water is the feminine; like a woman's emotions, it is always moving, flowing, changing. The river's intention is to connect with Source, the Divine—the Ocean. If the river is damned or log-jammed, the water (feminine) can be very destructive. It needs to flow.

How clear is your water? Is it clean or dirty, swift-flowing or slow-moving? Are you expressing your emotions?

Another analogy for this is in our physiology. The masculine aspect is the blood vessels and the feminine is the blood that runs through the vessels. The vessels give direction and structure for the blood to flow. We all know what happens if a vessel gets blocked or ruptured: we are in deep trouble. The blood's intention is to get back to the heart after it nourishes the rest of the body. The heart center is our connection to Source—the Divine.

We each can create a blissful life when we learn to balance our inherent masculine and feminine attributes. Heart is the feminine. The heart gives and receives love. It knows what we desire and are passionate about. Head is the masculine. It knows how to create what the heart desires. It gives

SECRET 12
The Feminine Principle – Doorway to Enlightenment

the direction and structure to the intention of the heart. Use heart-guidance to set your intentions, and let your masculine energy make a plan to bring your desires to fruition.

Sexual energy is the energy of creation; thus, it is feminine. It needs expression in a loving way. This expression becomes an emotional one; it wants to move to the heart. The sexual energy (feminine) fills the body container (masculine), which allows the sexual energy to move within it.

In Tantra, we fill our body containers with sexual energy. When the container is full, we can experience full body orgasms. We desire or long for orgasms because in that moment we connect with Source. The more we are orgasmic with life, the more we are connected to Source and the more we experience love and an open heart.

Most women have more feminine energy and can easily experience full body orgasms. Men can do this, too, when they learn a new way of being. We are all on our way to enlightenment. When we can achieve three hours of orgasmic energy, it can take us into enlightenment.

When we turn our lust (it doesn't have to be sexual lust; it can be lust for power, lust for money, lust for fame, lust for sleep, etc.) to love (coming from our hearts and Source) and love into prayer (the expression of the divine in all we do), we become enlightened.

The feminine energy wants to express unconditional love.

Sacred Sex, Sacred Life
JANET LEE

By moving sexual energy to our hearts, we can remember how to open our hearts.

> "Think before thou speakest."
>
> — CERVANTES
> *DON QUIXOTE DE LA MANCHA,*
> *PART IV, BOOK 3.*

SECRET 13

Conscious, Loving Communication

> "WHEN WE CLEARLY EXPRESS OUR EMOTIONS OR FEELINGS, OUR NEEDS AND WHAT IS "ALIVE IN US," WE CAN OVERCOME MANY PROBLEMS AND DIFFICULTIES IN OUR LIVES. LEARNING TO IDENTIFY OUR EMOTIONS AND OUR NEEDS IS SIMPLE BUT NOT EASY. FIRST WE GET IN TOUCH WITH OURSELVES; THEN WE GET IN TOUCH WITH OTHERS."
>
> —WWW.SECRETSOFTANTRA.COM

Charles and Caroline Muir, who wrote *Tantra: the Art of Conscious Loving*, state in their chapter on Tantric communication:

Conscious loving requires conscious communication. This does not mean that you have to learn a new vocabulary…but it does mean that you must be aware of what you are saying and that you must learn a ritual method of communication with your partner. When you are hurt, or angry, or insecure, you need to communicate your feelings to your partner (bad feelings that aren't aired can become infectious in a relationship), but you need to watch

> *your words in doing so. You need to avoid blaming your partner for your own feelings.*

One way to help couples become closer and more connected is to get them to spoon (lay side by side like two spoons in a drawer) twice a day for a minimum of five to ten minutes, synchronizing their breath. If there is a disagreement, they can stop and lie down and spoon each other in silence and breathe together. Soon the charge has dissipated, and they can talk lovingly to each other again.

My partner and I have done this since we learned it, and it has made a huge difference in our relationship. We know this works, and it creates more love and connection between us. We then can have conversations where we both feel heard. We are each more willing to help the other and get our needs met.

I taught this to a very horny and lustful client. He claimed he wanted/needed to have sex with his wife several times a day. After 25 years of marriage, he couldn't understand why his wife was losing interest. He learned about spooning, what foreplay and love-play meant, and he became more interested in intimacy. Now he can spoon with his wife while not getting so aroused and enjoy the connection they have. He uses this when they are having a spat and he reports an incredible improvement in their

Secret 13
Concious, Loving Communication

relationship. He is very grateful to have been taught this way of communicating.

More than speaking, the key to effective communication is listening. Many of us really don't know how to listen to our partners or to other people. There are two aspects of listening: One is awareness. The other is what we do with the "listening" or the way our "listening" impacts others. Listening is not passive. It has three levels of listening that I learned in my coaching classes from the book *Co-Active Coaching* by Laura Whitmore, Karen and Henry Kimsey-House, and Philip Sandahl.

Level one is self-centered listening. Our awareness focuses on ourselves. We listen to the words of the other person, but apply it to ourselves personally. There exists only one question: What does it mean to *me*? Level one listening informs us about ourselves and what's going on around us. It's where we relate what we hear to our own experience. When another person is sharing and you are caught up in your own thoughts, comparing what they say to your experience or devising (or even offering) your response before they have finished, you are only half-listening to the person who is speaking, making them feel insignificant.

For example, when someone is sharing about a trip they

took, be conscious and notice if you interrupt and trump them with your own travel story.

(This is my weakness. I interrupt when people are speaking. I am painfully aware of this, and I am slowly learning to zip up my mouth.)

Level-two listening requires giving full attention to the other person. Undisturbed by inner thoughts or the outside world, you offer a level of empathy, clarification, and collaboration. You focus your awareness totally on him or her—the words, the expressions, the emotions, everything he/she brings. When you allow the person to finish and speak only to ask for clarification, you are a perfect mirror for them. When you give another your full attention, that person usually feel heard and honored. One client felt so honored when she finally got to say what she needed to say, she cried and laughed and felt on top of the world. No one had ever heard her share her story. Once it was out, true healing took place.

Level-three is global listening. It is as though you and the other person are the center of the universe, receiving information from everywhere at once—like a radio-wave force field. You allow the environmental sounds to be part of the conversation. This type of listening calls for greater access of your intuition. When I am coaching a person and a fire truck siren is whaling in the background, I will ask

SECRET 13
Concious, Loving Communication

what alarms are going off in their lives.

Marshall Rosenberg, PhD, author of *Non-Violent Communication: A Language of Life*, says,

> *When people can get over their diagnosis of each other, their judgments, evaluations, criticisms, and connect to what is going on in each other, conflicts which seemed impossible to resolve seem to almost dissolve into nothingness.*

My Tantra teacher encourages us to learn non-violent communication (NVC) from Rosenberg. Non-violent communication is a language of compassion. Our words have the power to create profound healing or incredible suffering; yet, even with the best of intentions, it is often difficult to express ourselves in ways that build harmony and trust. Rosenberg explains:

> *What is alive in us? What brings us passion? What creates energy to feel alive? What makes every cell in your body dance with excitement and love?*
>
> *…NVC guides us in reframing how we express ourselves and hear others. Instead of habitual, automatic reactions, our words become conscious responses based firmly on an awareness of what we perceive, feel, and want. We are led to express ourselves with honesty and clarity while simultaneously paying others a respectful and empathic attention. The form is simple, yet powerfully transformative.…*

There are four components of the NVC Process:

1. *Observation*
2. *Feeling*
3. *Needs*
4. *Request*

First we observe what is actually happening in a situation: what are we observing others saying or doing that is either enriching or not enriching our life? The trick is to be able to articulate this observation without introducing any judgment or evaluation – to simply say what people are doing that we either like or don't like.

Next, we state how we feel when we observe this action: hurt, scared, joyful, amused, irritated, etc.

Third, we say what needs of ours are connected to the feelings we have identified.

The fourth component—a very specific request—addresses what we are wanting from the other person that would enrich our lives or make life more wonderful for us.[15]

A truck driver friend heard about this NVC, and he used it successfully at work. One day, the dispatch man was yelling at him over the two-way radio system. All the other men could hear this conversation. The truck driver followed

---

15. Marshall B. Rosenberg. *Non-violent Communication: A Language of Life,* Second Edition. (Encinitas, CA: PuddleDancer Press Book 2003).

SECRET 13
Concious, Loving Communication

the process. He simply said nicely that he didn't like being yelled at and asked what was wanted (Step 1). He told the dispatcher that he felt disrespected (Step 2). Then he expressed that he needed to be talked to as an adult (Step 3). And he made a clear request, "Wayne, would you be willing to stop yelling at me over the radio?" (Step 4). The result: Wayne was shocked to find it opened up the conversation. They came to an agreement that met both their needs.

Another way to communicate is with the Bradshaw Model I learned in Health and Wellness Coaching. One student, R.T., shared these 5 steps with us:

1. I Saw and/or Heard—Video camera or external view

2. I Interpreted—Personal filters and beliefs affecting my point of view

3. I Feel/Felt—Sharing true feelings without blame

4. I Learned—What I learned about myself and what new choices I am willing to make

5. I Want—Creation of a solution, new actions and choices

When we come from our hearts and connect with the heart of another, we create harmony and joy in our lives and enrich the lives around us.

In my own life, when I speak from my heart, the other person's heart hears, feels, and responds. We experience a heart-to-heart connection. It is like attracting bees to honey. Being able to speak up and request what I need, without going into emotion or drama, has improved my relationships with all people and resulted in wonderful outcomes that would have otherwise devolved into unpleasant situations. Facing one's fear to speak up is a huge opportunity for growth. It takes us out of our comfort zone, and we grow into loving human beings.

My clients are learning how they, too, can speak to their partners so that they will be heard. Practice this. The more you do it, the easier it gets.

Tantra requires of its students a certain level of awareness to avoid the disharmony that results from thoughtless communication. Start consciously speaking from your heart, and a whole new world of love and light will open to you.

Tantric practitioners know they can never make another person happy, but they can supply their intimate partner with many reasons to feel happy and loved. This is considered a sacred duty of each partner. Indulge one another every day with gifts of love, one of those gifts is loving communication.

> "By concentrating the ecstatic forces within, wonderful visions dawn in the mind's eye.
>
> This is a special secret, which shortens the journey to Liberation"
>
> —YOGINI TANTRA

CONCLUSION

This book covered just a few of the secrets to lead you toward a blissful life. It provides the basics of great living and loving. Also, I have introduced you to just a few of the principles I use in my practice and teachings. My observation has been that most people want to be better, more connected lovers.

When we speak with clear intentions and express from our hearts with love, miracles and magic can happen. Tantra has a plethora of rituals to bring you into conscious awareness. Here is a summary of tips to follow and put into practice:

1. Be willing to be loving and come from your heart. Turn your lust into love.

2. Be present in this moment in your life and especially when you are making love. Totally focus on body sensations: yours and those of your partner.

3. Do things that you enjoy doing. It revives your energy so you can bring newness and joy into any relationship.

4. Keep your body temple fit and healthy like a beautiful steed. Eat well, exercise, move, hydrate. Remember, it's the only one you get, and it is the vessel for your soul. Treat it with reverence. When we feel attractive, we are attractive; we have more confidence in our life and lovemaking.

5. Create a special place for your lovemaking, and keep it sacred. The energy builds over time, and it becomes a temple for love.

6. Find ways to defuse and de-stress your body and mind. Meditate, walk, dance, talk, get a massage. Stress is a main trigger for disease and lack of sex drive, killing off sexual intimacy in the bedroom.

7. "Relax" is not a directive the members of our society heed very often. Relax, smile, and enjoy your life. Listen to quiet, relaxing music. Take some time alone for introspection and reflection.

8. Breathe. Inhale deeply. Feel the energy move around your body. Breathe with your partner and become more in sync with each other.

9. Squeeze your love muscle. Practice solo and with your partner during lovemaking. This is healthy for both sexes.

10. Men can practice loving, caressing touch to release the hormone oxytocin to heighten desire and enhance bonding for both themselves and their partners. They can perform all lovemaking with consciousness and affection, and she will respond lovingly in return. Slow down and enjoy each other. Make it a meditation, and use the moment of orgasm to empower each other.

11. Men can choose when they want to ejaculate with loving consciousness. It is recommended that you only ejaculate once out of every four times you make love. This will increase your energy and vitality. Do your best to stay connected to your partner in the after-play of lovemaking.

12. Women, choose to speak up and say what you need and want, especially when it comes to making love. Men cannot read your minds, and they really do want to please you.

13. Remember, there is nothing more important than your love and connection as a couple. Learn to listen to each other and speak in a loving, conscious way.

14. Tantra is an art. It takes practice and patience. Slow down, keep eye contact, touch in loving ways, and embrace the divine in each other and yourself.

Tantra is a way of being and a spiritual lifestyle. I have shared with you the simplest, easiest way possible to apply some of the principles in your life today. May you receive many blessings on your journey to harmony and bliss.

NAMASTE,
JANET LEE

Glossary

<u>Ankh</u> — A symbol of immortality. It is the cross with the round circle on the top. pg 121

<u>Anorgasmic</u> — the inability to achieve sexual orgasms

<u>Cells of Recognition</u> — When we don't recognize something, we have no cells of recognition. Once we know what that is we activate brain cells to create new cells of recognition. An example: you are planning to buy a new car. You decide on the color, make, and model. All of a sudden, you see that car everywhere, even though you hadn't noticed it before.

<u>Chakra</u> — Chakras are spinning energy wheels along the sushumna, or central channel of the subtle body.

<u>Dopamine</u> — A hormone that is created in a gland in the brain called the hypothalamus and is also the brain's sex center. Dopamine is our motivator hormone. Men have a larger hypothalamus than women.

<u>Egregore</u> — Artificial demons called egregores are created by our negative thinking and act as demanding children as we get older. They demand our attention and feeding with unhealthy negative thoughts.

<u>Lingam</u> — Lingam means the penis. In Sanskrit, it means the wand of love, not lust.

<u>Namaste</u> — A greeting or salutation: the Divine in me sees the Divine in you.

<u>Oxytocin</u> — A bonding and natural anti-depressant hormone is released when you are touched in a loving way such as light caressing. It will increase desire, especially in women.

<u>PC muscle</u> — The pubococcygeous, or PC muscle, is a group of important pelvic floor muscles that run from your pubic bone (pubo) in the front, to your tailbone or coccyx (coccygenus) in the back. These muscles form the sling that holds up the bladder, uterus, or prostate gland.

<u>Sanskrit</u> — Ancient language

<u>Sushumna</u> — The invisible energy tube that runs along the spine from the top of the crown to the base or perineum.

<u>Squatters</u> — That is a term used when we leave an empty house or piece of land and an unauthorized individual occupies it in our absence.

<u>Tantra</u> — A Sanskrit word that has many meanings. One is: *TAN* — to extend *TRA* — self. Another one is to weave two different things together into union of one.

<u>Yoni</u> — Yoni means the female genitalia. In Sanskrit, it means the sacred garden, flower, altar or space.

<u>Yab-yum</u> — is the ultimate Tantra position. You sit cross-legged facing each other with the lighter partner sitting on the top of the partners lap.

Bibliography

Avinasha, Bodhi. *The Ipsula Formula: A Method for Tantra Bliss.* Valley Village, CA: Ipsula Publishing, 2003.

Bodansky, Steve, and Vera Bodansky. *Extended Massive Orgasm: How You Can Give & Receive Intense Sexual Pleasure.* Alameda, CA: Hunter House, 2000.

Carter-Scott, Cheri. *If Life is a Game, These are the Rules: Ten Rules for Being Human as introduced in Chicken Soup for the Soul.* New York: Broadway Books, 1998.

Chang, Stephen Thomas. *The Tao of Sexology: The Book of Infinite Wisdom.* Reno, NV: Tao Publishing, 1986.

Chia, Mantak, Maneewan Chia, Douglas Abrams, and Rachel Carlton Abrams. *The Multi-Orgasmic Couple: How Couples Can Dramatically Enhance Their Pleasure, Intimacy, and Health.* New York: Harper, 2000.

Chia, Mantak and Douglas Abrams Arava. *The Multi-Orgasmic Man: How Any Man Can Experience Multiple Orgasms and Dramatically Enhance His Sexual Relationship.* New York: Harper San Francisco, 1996.

Effendi, Irmansyah. *Reiki Tummo: An Effective Technique for Health and Happiness.* U.S.A: Yayasan Padmajaya, 2004.

Emoto, Masaru. *The True Power of Water: Healing And Discovering Ourselves.* Hillsboro, Oregon: Beyond Words Publishing, 2005.

Lacroix, Nitya. *The Art of Tantric Sex.* New York: DK Publishing, 1997.

Long, Barry. *Making Love: Sexual Love the Divine Way.* Los Angeles: Barry Long Books, 2006.

Muir, Charles, and Caroline Muir. *Tantra: the Art of Conscious Loving*. San Francisco: Mercury House, 1989.

Osho. *Body Mind Balancing: Using Your Mind to Heal Your Body*. New York: St. Martin's Griffin, 2003.

Osho. *Book of Secrets: 112 Keys to the Mystery Within*. New York: St. Martin's Griffin, 1994.

Osho. *Sex Matters: From Sex to Superconsciousness*. New York: St. Martin's Griffin, 2002.

Pauli, Michelle. *Sex with Spirit: An Illustrated Guide to Techniques and Traditions*. Boston, MA / York Beach, ME: Red Wheel, 2002.

Pease, Allan, and Barbara Pease: *Why Men Don't Listen & Women Can't Read Maps*. London: Orion Publishing, 2006.

Richardson, Diana. Tantric Orgasm for Women. Rochester, Vermont: Destiny Books, 2004.

Robinson, Marnia. *Peace between the Sheets: Healing with Sexual Relationships*. Berkley, CA: Frog, Ltd., 2004.

Roop, Shawn. Tantra Quest: *Tantric Counselor Handbook Level 1*, www.tantraquest.com, 2005

Rosenberg, Marshall B. *Non-violent Communication: A Language of Life*, Second Edition. Encinitas, CA: PuddleDancer Press Book, 2003.

Saraswati, Sunyata and Bodhi Avinasha. *Jewel in the Lotus: The Tantra Path to Higher Consciousness*, 3rd Edition. U.S.A.: Ipsula Publishing, 2002.

Solara, Lara, Dana da Ponte, and Marlene Chapman. *Universal Laws of Conscious Creation: Wisdom Book*. Canada: One House Publishing, 2008.

Whitworth, Laura, Karen Kimsey-House, Henry Kimsey-House, and Phillip Sandahl. *Co-Active Coaching: New Skills for Coaching People toward Success in Work and Life*, 2nd Edition. Mountain View, CA: Davies-Black Publishing, 2007.

About the Author

Janet Lee is a Transformational Goddess and Intimacy Coach.

She says her purpose is to help people transform physically, emotionally, and spiritually into a blissful life through conscious living and loving.

Over the past 24 years, she has been a holistic massage therapist. She is also a Reiki Master and has studied reflexology, herbology, iridology, aromatherapy, hypnotherapy, creative journaling, expressive arts, touch for health, craniosacral therapy, hot stone massage, BodyMind counselling, Tantra, spiritual healing, Sexological bodywork, LifeSuccess consulting, health and wellness coaching, and Tummo Reiki with open heart. With all this training, she received a Master of Science degree in Holistic Health with greatest distinction. She uses everything she has learned and integrates it into her massage work and teachings.

She feels blessed to have so many people come into her life and honored to witness their wonderful and beautiful transformations.

For more information about Courses, Classes, or Sessions

visit www.secretsoftantra.com or

Contact

Janet Lee

JanetLee@SecretsofTantra.com

Janet Lee invites your letters and comments about how the book has affected your life.

Order Today

Online orders: www.TendrilPress.com

Mail Postal Orders to:
 Tendril Press, LLC PO Box 441110 Aurora, CO 80044

Quantity orders please call: 303.696.9227

The price of each book is $14.95 plus applicable taxes.

Discounts available for quantity orders
 USA shipping —$3.50 for the first book,
   + $1.50 for each additional book.
 International shipping is $10.00 for the first book,
   $5.00 for each additional book,
US Check or Major Credit Cards accepted.

Card number: _____

Name on card: _____

Exp. Date: _____CVC2 Code: _____

Signature: _____

Telephone: _____

Ship to:

 Name: _____

 Address: _____

 City: _____ State: ___ Zip: _____

 Email Address: _____

 Telephone: _____

New Releases and Top Sellers
from Tendril Press

Tendril Press, LLC, is an Independent Press,
publishing thought provoking, inspirational, educational
and humanitarian books for adults and children.
Our highly-selective process is paying off, with multiple
award-winning books and an accepted entry for the Pulitzer Prize
We are changing lives worldwide, one book at a time.
Visit us often at *www.TendrilPress.com*
For Quantity orders of any title please call
303.696.9227